WORKING ON
WHAT MATTERS

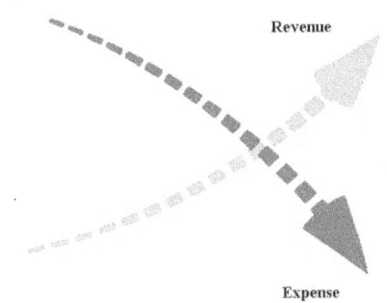

Revenue

Expense

the value analysis solution

DONALD E. PARKER

ISBN: 1481935542

ISBN 13: 9781481935548

Library of Congress Control Number: 2013900904
CreateSpace Independent Publishing Platform
North Charleston, South Carolina

Contents

Acknowledgments

In my first attempt to write this book I was just another boring engineer. My friend, Mary Ann Lewis, brought me back to life by suggesting that I spend two weeks reading other business books to understand current trends. I thank her for that, and hopefully she changed my style to that of a storyteller more interesting to all.

I am also grateful to the following members of the Value Engineering community who contributed their real-life examples used to produce this book. These examples demonstrate the diversity of the use of value analysis.

Michael P. Holt, PE, CVS, FSAVE
William L. Kelley, PE, CVS, FSAVE
Stephen J. Kirk, PhD, FAIA, LEED AP, CVS, FSAVE
Jill Woller, CVS, FSAVE
Tom Orr, PE, CVS
Wade Martin, CCC, CVS
Laurie Dennis, PE, LEED AP, CVS
Renee Hoekstra, CVS
Thomas F. Cook, CVS, FSAVE

My daughter, Katherine Rollins, must receive kudos for her editorial skills in keeping the book on theme by helping design the title, cover, and preface.

And of course my wife, Mary Frances, served as the consummate editor.

To the whole team — Thank you!

Preface

Through value analysis, the time and money you save might be your own.

In the face of declining revenue or increasing expenses — or both — you can use value analysis (VA) to work on both ends of the problem.

The *Washington Post* reported[1] the Commonwealth of Virginia was going to mandate a 4% budget cut in all departments across the board because of the impending fiscal cliff. The talk is that all federal agencies will take a 10% hit. It is tragic that these budget cuts are all they can think of doing.

Don't think fiscal problems are a one-time event. Most companies fail, and the government will always be out of money with the deficits they run. Barry Ritholtz[2] posted the failure rate of small businesses in their tenth year of operation as 35%.

In the years 2001 to 2010, 335 companies that were deemed to have a notable financial impact on the economy failed. Most failed from simple insolvency — ceasing operations following their inability to make a profit or to bring in enough revenue to cover their expenses.

According to Shikhar Ghosh, a senior lecturer at Harvard Business School: "If failing refers to failing to see the projected return on investment, then the failure rate is 70%-80%. If failure is defined as declaring a projection and then falling short of meeting it, then the failure rate is a whopping 90%-95%."

---

1 Metro Section, *Washington Post,* page B1, November 9, 2012.
2 Digital Media, Venture Capital, January 4, 2012.

This, however, need not happen. I tell stories of how executives use VA to improve processes and systems, to reduce waste and inefficiency, and to make budgeted dollars available for better use or debt reduction. I tell a story of how one major city enhanced its existing hospital revenues and one major utility reduced its expenses through the use of VA.

For more than six decades VA has contributed to profits and sales by improving the value of manufactured products, making the United States more competitive in the world. In the last four decades VA has been widely applied to improve the value of construction by staying within budgeted cost targets and achieving the return on investment desired.

Now is the decade of increasing emphasis on service industries in our economy. There is great need to improve business efficiency and government performance, and to minimize the cuts in service and loss that threatens each year.

VA can be applied to improve everything: organization, procedures, business practices, management systems, paperwork, information technology, services, and regulations. Many of these topics constitute the overhead cost of all fields of endeavor, such as labor, law, medicine, agriculture, education, housing, banking, finance, and business.

VA differs from other management practices because it is based on the analysis of functions, includes a multidisciplinary team approach, and follows a step-by-step process—a job plan that provides results in a short period of time.

Why not try out a technique that has proven its merit? This book will divert your attention from arbitrary cuts to working on what matters most through value analysis.

Donald E Parker, PE, CCE, CVS-Life, FSAVE

CHAPTER 1

The Solution in a Nutshell

If you do not change direction, you may end
up where you are heading.

- LAO TZU

Would you spend $50,000 to benefit a minimum of $500,000 with
a chance that the benefit could be $5 million? I'd bet that before
you put out that kind of money, you would need very positive
assurance that the method would work.

Well, it's not a trick. VA has always offered a ten-to-one
return on investment (ROI). VA will offer you at least ideas with
an ROI of twenty, betting that you will only accept half of the
ideas offered for change.

Rest assured, this is not a how-to book. You should hire a
consultant Certified Value Specialist (CVS)[3] for a professional

---

3 Refer to SAVE International Consultants Directory at website: http://www.
value-eng.org/professionals_directory.php

value study to ensure you do not get a cost-cutting study instead, which sacrifices needed functionality.

The nuance of what I just stated is important. Don't lose it!

Value is all about the worth of something, which involves money, but also much more. It also involves required performance and timeliness. For example, a drink of water to **quench thirst** in the desert is much more valuable than in a restaurant.

Cost reduction involves sacrifice of something you'd really like to have but at the moment cannot afford. That's what happens with arbitrary budget cuts. Cost reduction separates needs from desires—the need for transportation and the desire for a Rolls Royce.

Well-performed VA does not involve sacrifice.

✶✶✶

Here is the essence of the method. Lawrence D. Miles[4], father of VA, discovered long ago that "All cost is for function...all a customer wants is a function. He either wants something done or he wants someone pleased."

VA defines the functions of your products, systems, and procedures. A basic function is the primary purpose or most important action performed by a product, process, or service. A secondary function is a function that supports the basic function and results from the specific approach used to perform the basic function. All functions are expressed as **verb nouns**. In this text, functions are written in **bold** text to identify them.

You allocate cost to those functions. Then you judge the worth of those functions to decide which functions are most in need of value improvement.

If we do the VA job right, we eliminate redundant functions or learn to perform necessary functions in another manner.

Since our economic measure of value is life-cycle cost, we use it to judge the quality of recommended changes. In that

---

4 Lawrence D. Miles, *Technique of Value Analysis and Engineering*, 3ʳᵈ *Edition* (The Lawrence D. Miles Value Foundation, 1989).

way we ensure no degradation to required performance or maintainability.

You might ask, how can this be? How can one method be applied to so many areas with success? The secret is so fundamentally simple that it takes some effort to master.

Value methodology is common to all because it deals with functions—and everything has a function. Two elements are therefore necessary to perform VA: the "problem" must be described in function terms, and the alternate approaches to achieve the functions must be valid considerations.[5]

Value Analysis (VA)
A structured multidisciplinary practice to analyze the functions of systems, designs, criteria, etc. to satisfy needed quality and user requirements at optimal total cost of ownership.

---

5 A valid consideration is one that achieves all required performance over the life span of use at the quality level, operability, and maintainability desired.

CHAPTER 2

Solving Problems

We can't solve problems by using the same kind of
thinking we used when we created them.

- ALBERT EINSTEIN

I'll never forget the day I started as manager for an agency
wanting a VA program. As any new employee, I wanted to get
off to a good start and be helpful and useful to my new employer.

The best way I thought to do this was to work on what they
wanted worked on. So I sent a memo around to all the department heads asking for them to submit their five most pressing
problems. I would then prioritize them, gather up employee
teams, teach them VA, and get to work recommending solutions
to their problems. To hell with focusing on savings — that would
come later. This would be useful work!

To my chagrin — and showing my naiveté — no one had any problems. At least, none were submitted. No one would admit to any
problems, which sent a strong message to "stay out of my business."

***

In addition to being a technique for identifying unnecessary cost, the VA method is a problem-solving system. It can be used to solve problems regardless of the cost of the solution. Therefore, application of the technique in itself does not necessarily mean that money will be saved. There are five ways value can be improved as shown by the following diagram:

Value Improvement

P = Performance (Benefits)   C = Cost (Life-Cycle Costs)

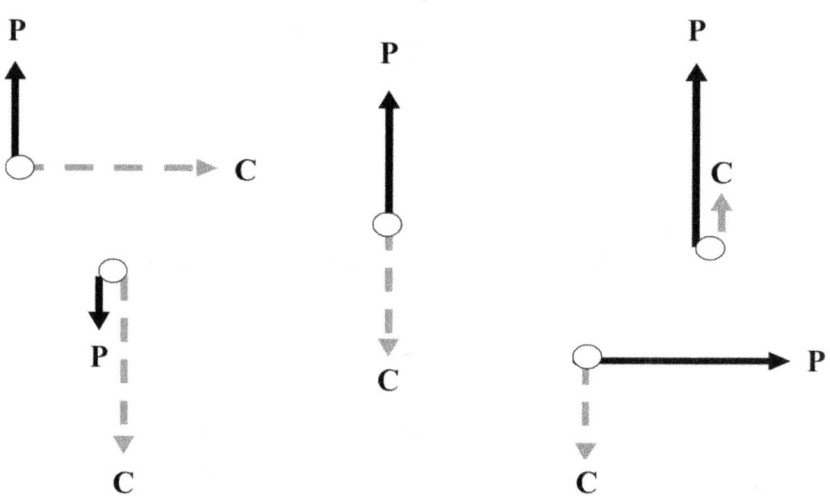

Value is improved when performance goes up while cost remains the same, when performance goes up while cost goes down, when performance increases more than cost increases, when cost decreases more than performance decreases, and when cost decreases while performance remains the same.

You can achieve a lot by performing VA at the concept-development stage and recognize the benefits of cost avoidance that may head off future fiscal cliffs.

***

I was dreaming at work one day about my plans of going to the Carillon Hotel in Miami Beach for the annual SAVE[6] conference. This would be a great time to combine work with play — something government workers could never do in these days with all the budget constraints. But I was the value program manager and had worked very hard to **have fun**.

My plan was to load the family onto the auto-train and arrive in Orlando with the kids in tow. We would spend a couple of days at Disney World and then send the kids up to Tallahassee to stay with Grandma while my wife and I went off to Miami.

I thought this a great plan. After all, Tallahassee was only 244 miles from Orlando. It was less than thirty minutes by airplane on a direct, one-way flight. Grandma would be waiting at the airport for them, and we would be free for four whole days!

Larry Miles, the father of value analysis, always spoke of how VA was a problem-solving technique. I was eager to try it out. My problem was to **sell family** on my plan. After all, we didn't have a lot of money, I didn't want to seem extravagant, and I had to use some vacation time. We would be making this trip instead of traveling to the beach to frolic.

So, one evening I gathered my wife and our children—then ages 8 and 5—around the dining room table as my task team. Even though we had only four team members (the recommended number at the time being five) we did have a round dining room table, which is better for eye contact than a square or rectangular table.

As I announced my plan and explained the magic of Orlando's Disney World, the kids responded enthusiastically. Yaaay—they wanted to see Mickey Mouse! I didn't notice it at the time, but my wife sat back and kept quiet.

As a VA team leader I was taught to use good human relations, interface with all team members, and attempt to read their feelings in advance to pre-empt roadblocks. I did fail at this first lesson, which I will explain later.

---

6   Then the Society of American Value Engineers, now SAVE International

Oh boy, I thought, now was the time to apply function analysis. I asked the kids what we should do after all the fun at Disney World. Their answer was go **see Grandma**. Good job so far, I thought.

So I asked them what function would do that. How would we go **see Grandma?** After a little two-word prodding for an active verb and a measurable noun, I came up with a function: **transport livestock**.

I explained that the "transport" portion was to move them from Orlando to Grandma's (point A to point B), and the "livestock" portion was to ensure that they arrived in good shape (fed and alive). With that I thought the problem of **ditching kids** would be solved.

The kids jumped for joy. They said **transport livestock** was "like you put little doggies in a cage" to move them from place to place. They were spot on and would soon be good little value analysts. So we brainstormed a bunch of ideas. Some of the ideas I remember were:

- Hire a limousine
- Call a cab
- Get a policeman to take them
- Put them on a slow boat to the other side of Florida
- Ship them with FedEx (the cage concept)
- Escort them by plane
- Send them alone by plane
- Put them on a Greyhound bus
- Pay to have Grandma come get them in Orlando
- Drive them up in our car
- Rent another car and find someone to drive them up
- Use a train
- Get a truck driver to take them
- Leave them with a sitter in Orlando

I didn't know it at the time, but the methodology would bring out the real problem. The team was working on **transport livestock**, which was child's play. It wasn't the real problem.

My wife sat back during brainstorming and didn't contribute. This time I did sense something was wrong, but was clueless as to what it was.

Nevertheless, we went on to the evaluation phase. All of the ideas seemed to achieve the basic function **transport livestock** in one way or another. However, most of them presented one or more of the following problems: they cost more money rather than less, seemed more of a risk, or would take up more time than we wanted to take before we could get on down to Miami.

After performing a weighted evaluation of the alternatives, I announced the preferred solution: send them on the airplane alone from Orlando to Tallahassee, and have Grandma meet them at the airport.

With that, my wife spoke up. "You beast!" she said. "How dare you think of sending my babies alone on an airplane?"

I said in shock, "What do you mean?"

She said, "You cheapskate. How can you assure the safety of our children doing that?"

"You're right," I said. "Let's not discuss it further. I'll think of something else."

The lesson I learned from this is to never attempt to sell an idea without a strategy to implement it. But by this time I had to first, recover from being painted as a cheapskate before I could move another step toward implementation; and second, have a solid implementation strategy to immediately follow up my idea.

To overcome the cheapskate image, I had to show that I would spend money if that is what it took to achieve my wife's (the user's) function **assure safety**. So the next morning I went downtown to the airline office and purchased two round-trip tickets for the adults and two one-way tickets for the children between Orlando and Tallahassee.

I brought those four tickets home that evening and plunked them on the value workshop (dining room) table. "There," I said. "I did it! We can both escort our children to Grandma's to be sure they get there safely and then we can turn around and fly back to Orlando to pick up our car and go to Miami."

With that my wife said, "Wow! What did that cost?"

This was the opening to success that I wanted. "Who cares?" I said. "That is what you wanted so that is what I did!"

That moment was the time for the art of selling and to recoup my losses, so I continued: "However, the expense is not lost. If you have another idea that would work, we can return the tickets and get a refund. Otherwise, the trip is confirmed for us."

She said, "I hate to spend all that money just to go and turn around, and we are wasting one whole day flying before we have to drive to Miami."

At that moment I was ready with two additional implementation plans:

1. One of us could fly the kids to Tallahassee and return, while the other one waits at the airport all day. That would save the cost of one of the round-trip tickets.
2. We could go to the Orlando airport, meet a nice stewardess who would give the kids a badge (miniature wings), and chaperone them for free on the plane to Tallahassee. That would save the cost of both round-trip tickets.

If we chose the second option, we would wait at the Orlando airport until they arrived and call Grandma to make sure the children arrived safely. If they didn't, then we would use our tickets to Tallahassee to follow on the next airplane behind them. While we waited at the airport together we would **dine out** — starting our vacation alone by having a nice breakfast.

The offer to **dine out** was what sold the idea! And that is what we did. We saved the cost of both round-trip tickets and a full day wasted by flying and waiting.

Function-inspired change provided the communication tool we needed to form a group of disparate people into a team. VA facilitates the achievement of consensus needed to bring along even the most reluctant team member.

The kids had a wonderful time flying alone. The little one took the big one's hand and proudly led her onto the plane.

But upon arrival in Tallahassee, both children sat in their seats while passengers started to get off. The plane was scheduled to continue on to Baton Rouge.

After a short while the little one told her sister, "Come on. We have to get off. Grandma is waiting for us." With that she took her sister's hand and led her off the plane and down the ramp. She remembered I had told her to get off at the first stop the plane made.

Grandma later told us, "I was waiting at the bottom of the ramp. The plane wasn't going anywhere until I inspected it for the kids. So don't you worry."

Those were the good old days when one could be at the ramp of an arriving and departing aircraft. I wonder how it would work today with the TSA!

***

With budgets all up in the air, don't you think there is a ripe opportunity to define the function of travel for meetings, training, and conferences by applying VA to them? Managers could reduce the waste and still get the purpose accomplished.

CHAPTER 3

The Flavor of the Month

Here we go again—another program! But, listen up...

- DONALD PARKER, AUTHOR

In the 1970s, zero-based budgeting was in vogue. Everyone jumped through hoops doing it. I tried to no avail to get my agency to budget the functions they were to perform rather than just the personnel, activities, and tasks on hand.

The National Archives and Records Service was embracing and teaching work simplification techniques. I tried to get them to define the function of the work before simplifying work that might not be necessary in the first place.

In the 1980s, Management by Objectives (MBO) and Total Quality Management (TQM) were the craze. These days we have LEAN and Six Sigma to rely on as the latest techniques for managers.

Through all of these trends, value analysis has survived since the 1940s. It has proven itself to be consistently effective.

***

A major part of the responsibility of the head of any organization is to "protect and conserve" the resources entrusted to their use by investors or taxpayers. Doing this will help to ensure the survival of both public and private business.

The question then follows: how much effort and how many resources is one willing to allocate to this function, and under what methods does one wish to manage this activity? The methods available to managers to conserve and protect resources are many and varied. But basically, they can be put into two groups: static and dynamic.

Static methods are devices built into the process of doing business, such as guidelines, regulations, and laws. They occur all the time to protect investors and taxpayers, and they cost resources to achieve their benefit.

Static methods exist to regulate and prevent management from obvious waste, fraud, and abuse. However, the costs and benefits of adopting and implementing static methods are rarely calculated.

It is the dynamic methods for protecting and conserving resources that are really the subject at hand. These compete for the resources of management. They are dynamic for a number of reasons. First, their emphasis and utilization fluctuates with the seasons of changing leaders and power. Second, the level of their use by managers is limited by the managers' understanding, experience, training, and preconceived notions concerning these methods. Third, the level of their use by employees is limited by these same issues, in addition to the employees' perception of management's interest in the methods.

Below is a small sampling of the various types of static and dynamic methods in use today.

Operational — Mission-Related Responsibility
Conserve & Protect Resources

STATIC METHODS	DYNAMIC METHODS
Personnel Ceilings	Six Sigma
Budget Limitations	Work Simplification
Competitive Procurement	LEAN
Laws	Value Analysis
Regulations	Life-Cycle Costing
	Management by Objectives
	Employee Suggestions
	Zero-Based Budgeting
	Cost Reduction

Before discussing in more detail the selection of dynamic methods, let us address the perceptions that operating managers seem to have when it comes to allocating resources — ceiling, dollars, and workforce hours — to these types of functions. Understandably, they wonder about operational priorities, how their job will be made easier, who will get the credit, and what that credit is. Direct benefit to them is not apparent.

Perceived Program Impact

Action	Fear
Improve productivity	Reduced budget ceiling
Save money	Unobligated funds signal poor performance
Encourage suggestions	Increased workload
Generate LCC savings	Demands on limited money

| Encourage studies | Diluted operational performance |
| Identify problems | Reflects on job performance |

In the business world, the function of effort to protect and conserve resources is clear. It contributes to profit. And, both managers and employees can rationalize that what is good for the company is good for them.

In the public sector and nonprofit organizations, the function and purpose of the expected effort is more subtle. It is to improve the utilization of resources so more required work can get done within the available budget. Yet, the evaluation system for such organizations is often designed to create apprehension regarding impact on resources and performance instead of motivation to perform.

For example, when government agencies first pushed for the implementation of energy conservation, the following statement was included in its implementing report:[7]

"It is almost axiomatic that any effort or program is helped by top management interest. Human nature is such that most employee time and effort is directed toward those aspects of the job that are closely reviewed and about which management is concerned."

With regard to energy conservation, the report found there was an attitude that the mission of the activity was the total and top priority, and that conservation of energy was only a secondary function.

Most managers and employees do not perceive a direct "sense of duty" to assist in protecting and conserving resources because the effort required is not treated as a task assignment equal in importance to other mission or operational priorities.

***

---

7 Joint GSA-FEA-OMB, *Energy Conservation Site Visit Report (Conservation Paper Number 38)* April 1976.

Prevailing misconceptions and oversimplification act adversely on the effective use of many dynamic methods. Here are a few of the more common notions:

- Improved productivity is achieved only by working harder or faster.
- Work simplification results only by cutting out steps in the process.
- Management improvement benefits cannot be calculated.
- Energy conservation is an artificial problem.
- Cost reduction always means giving up something.
- Achieving life-cycle cost savings requires higher first costs.
- Management by Objectives requires commitments without resources.
- Management studies result only in reports.

These misconceptions can all be corrected through education and application. Regardless of the method used to conserve and protect resources, it is important that the effort desired first be a closely reviewed job responsibility. A good way to achieve this is to accept the task as an operational responsibility, commit resources to it, and manage those resources to ensure effective results.

***

When a specific method is promoted in an organization, the common argument is that another management practice is being demanded when the organization is already burdened with many worthwhile "programs."

The dictionary[8] defines a program as an "official edict or decree" and a "prearranged plan or course of proceedings." To carry this one step further, the dictionary defines an official edict as "a formal, written act." A pre-arranged plan is an arrangement of means or steps for the attainment of some objective which,

---

8 *The New Practical Standard Dictionary,* Funk & Wagnalls Company, 1956

when operational, has personnel assigned to accomplish the tasks, an operating budget, and measurable identified outputs.

Check your "programs" against the above five criteria. Most so-called programs fail to meet the definitional test of a program. Static methods are not budgeted. Dynamic methods often fail to measure up in one or more category.

For example, few employee "suggestion programs" have annual goals for receipt of suggestions, personnel time budgeted to review suggestions, or money set aside to pay awards. Management simply sits back passively and waits for employee participation. These occasions do not meet the test of a program definition.

Why favor value analysis? Because VA has the following:

- Universal application
- Support of all existing techniques
- Teachable methodology
- Usefulness to employees at all levels
- Improvement success rates
- Ability to pay for itself

Value analysis is a program as well as a methodology. It is a professional, deliberate way to conserve and protect resources by advocating change to improve value. VA is an active, not passive, approach.

VA is the only program with universal application in all of the other dynamic method areas. VA has the advantage of advocating, or concentrating on, no new techniques other than the relationship of cost and worth to function. It teaches and supports the application of all existing techniques to the proper problem.

***

Not all good ideas come from VA. Some managers get lucky — like finding fallen apples from a tree — and if they are smart, they use these ideas to improve their business. But when all is said and done, and you can think of no other way to improve or wring out more cost, then value analysis can step in and prove you wrong.

VA is one of the few known ways that you can study something with no apparent results in mind, and produce in a short time frame (one to two weeks) astounding ideas for improvement. These ideas become your opportunities for change. Don't let them end up in paper reports through inaction.

Studies that end in paper reports fail because they do not satisfy management. They often define the wrong problem, study the wrong issue, arrive at unworkable solutions, fail to have all the information, fail to be creative, lack empathy for implementation, or fail to quantify benefits. Value studies specifically address each of these issues as part of the methodology.

The function of VA is to improve value. Organizations can improve value by improving services, reducing paperwork, improving productivity, simplifying work, attaining required quality, conserving energy, achieving objectives economically, and auditing for problems and performance.

CHAPTER 4

What is it Worth?

An ounce of practice is worth more than tons of preaching

- MAHATMA GANDHI

Now that you have an idea as to what the value methodology is all about, the strategic part of performing VA is to work on what matters.

And what matters is the cost of those functions that you know are not worth their cost. That is what we call a value mismatch that provides you with an opportunity for improvement.

However, be warned. The worst thing you can do is tell someone exactly what their product, item, or system is worth. Avoid that mistake.

It is much better to allocate cost to function, and know for sure from experience that the function shouldn't cost that much. Then you can speak up. You have discovered a value mismatch.

When the cost of **find information** takes four hours, you know that can be improved. When the newspaper indicates an agency's time to **admit wounded warriors** takes 434 days, you know that can be improved.

✳✳✳

Determining the worth of a function is a matter of judgment. It is done through:

- Personal experience
- Comparison with another function
- Use of historical data
- Benchmarking

Compare the present way of performing the function with other methods of performing essentially the same function.

For example, I was involved with ordering doors for the x-ray room of an air force hospital at a cost of more than $750 each. The function of the door was to **restrict view** of the occupant inside. Immediately I thought of a function equivalent—a drapery used in a local department store where people tried on clothing. The worth of the **restrict view** function quickly became $100 and a prime candidate for value improvement.

The $750 soundproof doors with locking hardware provided unnecessary function. What were the people going to do in there?

The rule is: determine the cost of a functional equivalent based upon the way it has been previously accomplished. To aid in determining worth, ask the following questions:

- What is the cost of achieving the basic function as presently being performed?
- Do you think the performance of the basic function should cost that much?
- If not, what do you consider would be a reasonable amount to pay for the performance of the function (assuming for the moment that the function is actually required) if you were to pay for it out of your own pocket?

- What is the cost of achieving this function if some other known method is used?
- Is this a common, easily accomplished function or one that is rare and difficult to achieve?
- What is the price of some method that will almost — but not quite — perform the function?

I cannot say it too often: in determining worth, the key rule to be remembered is that worth is associated with necessary functions and not with the method or system.

Carlos Fallon[9] relates a story to illustrate this rule. A sophisticated task team was trying to define the function of a washing machine hose (cost: $.25) in order to determine its worth. A youngster who happened to be there said, it **bends water**. The team accepted that definition of function and sent the boy out to a hardware store to help determine worth by purchasing the cheapest water bender he could find.

The boy came back with a plumbing "U," which at that time cost $.05. However, the pipe was heavy and ugly. So the team's purchasing man called a plastic supplier who, for another $.03 could make it lighter and softer, and for another $.04 could make it pretty. The worth of **bending water** thus became $.12.

Some value specialists give worth only to basic functions, automatically letting the worth of secondary functions be zero. This view is taken because to some, secondary functions only exist because of the solution used to satisfy the basic functions. Hence, when an alternative way to satisfy the basic functions is discovered, all the old, secondary functions drop out of existence.

✻✻✻

Forms, forms, forms. All through my life I've experienced worthless forms that everyone wants to have filled out.

The worst one ever was the Request for Training form my agency used. It was a legal-sized form so long and onerous that I

---

9 Carlos Fallon, *Value Analysis, 2nd revised edition* (The Lawrence D. Miles Value Foundation, 1980).

asked my secretary to fill one out for me while I was on a trip to California. At least it wouldn't waste my precious time.

I told her it had to be sent in early for registration so I could get the $100 discount offered by the course. When I returned a week later, I received the bad news from my secretary. It hadn't been submitted.

One of the spaces on the form to be filled out—other than my name, employee number, Social Security number, grade level, office, division, job title, name of the course, supplier of the course, cost, etc.—was my birth date. She did not have that information. So like a dutiful and responsive person, she called the personnel office to find out my birthday.

Well, the Privacy Act of the Federal Government was staring them in the face. It would not let them tell her my birthday so she could complete the form. She next tried to call my wife, who was not at home. She even called my mother-in-law, who was clueless. So the uncompleted form was never submitted.

I was furious, and I asked, "What is the function of putting my birth date on the form? If I am too young does it mean I can't have training? If I am too old are they discriminating?"

It was then that I realized the form had an overall function—**approve training,** as evidenced by the permission given by the signature of my supervisor—but that each block to fill in on the form also had a function.

Upon closer examination of the form I noticed there was a block of space for the insertion of accounting data to pay for the training. This too, was stupid. The form did not **obligate funds**. After it was signed it had to go up to Finance where they filled out another form to **obligate funds**.

There were so many unnecessary and redundant secondary functions being asked on the form that it could have easily been reduced from legal size to letter size without sacrificing the basic function of **approve training** one iota. This would also have the benefit of fitting into our copy machines much better.

I figured the cost of my secretary filling out the form that was never submitted was four hours of time, with a worth of no more than ten minutes. But there was also the cost of legal-sized paper for the whole agency, plus the $100 savings for early enrollment that was lost. You can imagine what the overall worth of that Request for Training form was for the whole organization.

***

As the above examples show, worth can be established at various levels of detail.

At the component level of a large system, one might judge the least cost of the various functions provided by a report. For example, the questions:

- What is the least cost to **send information**? Use the phone.
- What is the least cost to **store information**? Use a thumb drive.

All of these, and others, are functions of a report.

At a system level, one frequently has available parameter costs and can put a temporary cost on such things as the cost per person served or cost per report received until creative VA effort establishes the worth of the functions.

Both public- and private-sector managers can use indicators of "function worth" from sources such as financial ratios, bench-marking, and capitalized-income analysis.

***

My good friend Gary and his wife had a condo at the beach, and realized that it was a wasting asset. The condo rent broke even with its expenses, and brought in very little profit. He knew that he could put the proceeds to better use by paying off credit card debts as they entered retirement, and they could live on their Social Security benefits and his government pension.

He had been trying to sell the condo for almost three years, with no takers from 2008–2011 because of the economy. So he went to his bank to see if he could take out a loan on the condo until it was sold.

The bank vice president reviewed their application and thought everything looked OK. They were putting up an asset with a value of more than four times the loan amount. The bank went ahead and had an appraisal done on the condo.

My friends thought they were home free until some unknown reviewer at the bank denied the loan at the last minute. It was denied based upon Gary's indicator of worth at the bank. It was called the debt-to-income ratio. Just a few years ago one could get a loan with no job, no income, no references, nothing! Not now. The bank's loan reviewer cited Gary's credit card debt as the excuse to deny the loan.

"Of course," Gary said. "The loan was to pay off the credit card debt owed so that my debt-to-income ratio would be lower." The bank representative even told him that he and his wife would receive no money—the bank would pay off the credit cards directly.

In pressing the bank further, he found that they did not count any money from rent, interest, dividends, stock, retirement plans, gifts, or self-employment income as "income" because it was unreliable. They only counted Social Security income and pension.

However, the bank did include the taxes, fees, utility bills, and telephone bill on the condo as "debt." How unfair, when the rental income couldn't be used to offset the debt.

This was a real chicken-and-egg runaround problem that needed to be tackled. Gary told me his story and asked for help in exploring alternative ways to **obtain funds**. I told him we needed better information on ways to **obtain funds** and persistence to get the job done.

As Calvin Coolidge said, "Nothing in the world can take the place of persistence,

Talent will not; nothing is more common than unsuccessful men with talent,

Genius will not; unrewarded genius is almost a proverb,

Education will not; the world is full of educated derelicts,

Persistence and determination alone are omnipotent. The slogan "Press On" has solved and always will solve the problems of the human race."

So we conducted an in-person survey of all the banks in the area to **obtain funds**. We told each one the experience with the first bank. We received all kinds of ideas on how they could help Gary if they could get his business. One bank even said that if he opened a brokerage account with them for $200,000, they would loan him $100,000.

That was our Ah-ha! moment. Gary had a brokerage account — why did he need another? Well, he didn't. He went to his broker with his wife and in one day they wired $100,000 to his account at the bank that originally refused him. He paid off his credit cards and had some to spare.

What they got was a margin loan that has an interest rate one-half of what he was paying on the credit cards — 7 percent in lieu of an average of 14 percent. But the best thing is they eliminated their monthly credit card bill. And they need never pay back the margin loan; the monthly dividend and interest sweep in their brokerage account pays it back. And a margin loan doesn't count as "debt," which only seems fair because the dividends and interest from the stock don't count as "income."

For a really happy ending, now with a good debt-to-income ratio, they now could refinance their house to take advantage of the lower mortgage rates before the national financial cliff goes away. Some good has to come out of all of this.

Their only regret is that they didn't do it all three years earlier. They would have saved $21,000 in interest.

✳✳✳

I also like to determine worth by taking published, historical data and transforming normally used statistical parameters to create cost data. For example, you can create the cost of a medical staff on a cost-per-patient-day basis. Casting a new light on foregone and accepted cost data often poses startling results.

On a hospital study I once conducted, our professional hospital consultant on the team provided the following benchmarks:

> Computer staffing – 31 people per 650 beds
> Computer terminals – 1 per 2 beds
> Computer operators – 9 per 400 beds
> Response time – 1 to 3 seconds at peak
> Downtime – 45 minutes per day, scheduled
> Downtime – 2 hours per month, unscheduled

This data was used to recommend computerization of patient records to eliminate the long wait patients encountered when registering at the hospital, and to show the benefits of implementing the VA study.

✳✳✳

Capitalized-income analysis has been used for many years by the private sector as an investment-analysis technique to evaluate the economics of business decisions. In VA, understanding this approach can provide an overall indicator or worth of the function of a project. The technique can be used to:

- Identify requirements that exceed the value expected from equivalent commercial income
- Reduce budgets for systems and projects so that cost more nearly equals worth
- Establish the financial relationship between income and cost for each proposed expenditure

If the desire is to achieve a certain return-on-investment (ROI), then performing VA to prevent cost overruns is a must.

The income approach centers on the thesis that value is "the present worth of future rights to income." This method requires one to determine the revenues — real or imputed — that may reasonably be anticipated during the estimated economic life of the system. Gross income is reduced to net income, and then capitalized (discounted) at a market rate of interest including recapture (capitalization rate), which reflects the quantity, certainty, and quality of the anticipated income "stream." This approach is represented by the generic equation:

$$\text{system value} = \frac{\textbf{net income}}{\textbf{capitalization rate}}$$

The capitalization rate — also known as the going rate of interest, cost of money, or market rate of interest (plus recapture provisions)—constitutes a ratio of income-to-market value for the system. For projects, the author uses the following formula, which simply states that most systems require initial capital investment and borrowed capital.

$$\text{system value} = \frac{\text{net income}}{(1\text{-}K)\,(ROR) + K\,(CRF)}$$

K   = ratio of borrowed funds to total cost
ROR   = rate of return desired
CRF   = capital recovery factor—amount to pay back a one dollar loan with interest over a specified term, at a constant annual payment

This type of analysis can be applied to all forms of investment even though the owner/user is not actually receiving income. The basis of capitalization can be imputed income using avoided expenditures. For example:

Type of Investment	Possible methods for computing income
Motor pool operation	Rental car income
Prison	Cost-per-prisoner to house them elsewhere
Employment system	Use of executive search firm
Payroll system	Cost to contract it out

Before spending capital for any system or project, the value of the budgeted amount can be checked against its economic worth.

***

One of the best places for determining worth is at the concept stage of system development. For example, in one instance a billing system was proposed for a company that would cost $40,000 per year to operate.

Although the billing system was a comparatively small fish in a large pond, it was worth a quick challenge. In a flash, the value specialist related the cost of the function **generate invoice** as $400 (based on 100 invoices per year for the company), and the worth of the function **generate invoice** as no more than $25. The cost of the function was related to the cost of the time for one person doing the job on a typewriter, which served as the basis for judging worth of the function. Immediately, potential for a value study was uncovered.

In many cases, when conducting a value study, various levels of indenture of verb–noun functions will be suggested automatically as the basic function of an item or system. A diverse study team is bound to do this.

For example, if you were to study the Supplemental Nutrition Assistance Program (SNAP) and ask the team to define the basic function of the program, they may list the following functions:

- **Improve life**
- **Feed people**
- **Distribute food**
- **Distribute cards**

Are all of these basic functions of the program? Depending on point of view, they probably are. Which function would you choose to assign a cost and worth to, and then develop alternatives for? Obviously, you would get very different ideas depending upon the function you selected, and the scope of your study would vary drastically. What has just been illustrated is a problem in level of indenture, or the hierarchy of functions.

The significance of a level of indenture is that the designation of function as basic or secondary depends upon the indenture level selected. A function that exists to support the method of performing the basic function is a secondary function. But when considered by itself, and with respect to itself, it is a basic function.

CHAPTER 5

Function-Inspired Change

The journey of discovery begins not with new vistas but
with having new eyes with which to behold them

- MARCEL PROUST

Defining everything with verbs and nouns are the new eyes that
many are unaccustomed to using. Most people don't think that
way.

Who runs to the grocery store when they run out of beer and
then stops in the middle of the aisle to ask, "What am I doing?"
Then, if the answer is **quench thirst**, do you stop and ask yourself, "Why beer? What alternatives are there to quenching thirst?"

If the higher-order function you are really trying to achieve
is **impress date**, you might go for the wine or champagne. If it is
improve health, you might head for the milk or orange juice. If
it is **reduce cost**, go for the water or soda. If it is **get drunk**, keep
on heading toward the beer. All of the above drinks will **quench
thirst** to some degree.

Many people say they do value analysis all the time but have no concept of what that really means. Sure, my wife goes to the grocery to **obtain protein** all the time. I just never know what she'll bring back and whether or not she will allocate cost per ounce to the function.

When I first went to work I did all sorts of design reviews, suggested many changes, saved the agency lots of money, and counted it as VA savings with the U.S. Navy auditor to meet our annual goals. But was it really VA if it didn't involve that function thing?

I was too new to the program to have experienced the function epiphany—creating change—and wasn't really quite sure how that worked.

Then one day I got my chance. It was the fall of 1966, and the newly designed enlisted men's barracks for the Naval Medical Center in Bethesda, Maryland had just come in 24.3% over budget.

The budget had been set by Congress at a statutory limit of $1,850 per person. So, for our 360-person building we had just $666,000 to spend on construction. Unfortunately the low bid came in at $828,000 or $2,300 per person. This doesn't seem like a lot, but in those days it was.

Our captain, the commanding officer of the Chesapeake Division of the Naval Facilities Engineering Command called all the design division branch managers into his conference room to discuss what to do about the situation. As the newly minted division value analyst, I was also invited.

The captain was lamenting the cost of obtaining qualified, Navy hospital corpsmen and the poor living conditions we provided them, which affected their retention rate. He nearly shouted, "Do you have to run fifty feet down the hall to go to the bathroom in the middle of the night? Why should they?"

Right then I thought of the corridor. It was wasted space we had to pay for. No one could sleep in or otherwise use the corridor. What was its basic function? Its basic function was to **connect space**.

I knew that a building like this should be 70% efficient (Net SF/Gross SF). And about 15% was being used to **connect space**, costing $125,000.

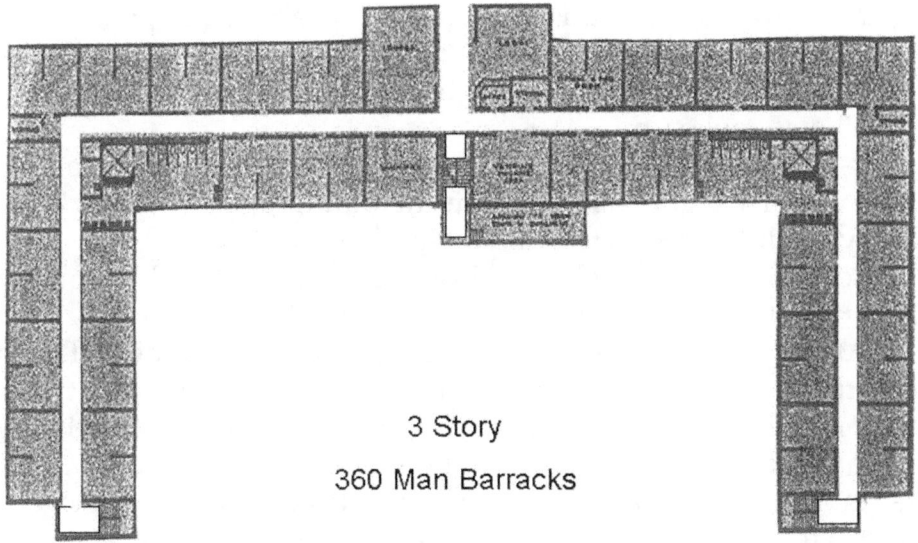

3 Story

360 Man Barracks

A secondary function for a corridor is to **guide egress**. The cost of that function involved fire-rated doors, panic hardware, exit lighting, emergency lighting, smoke control, fire-rated walls and ceilings, and enclosed pressurized stairwells at each end of the corridor. All of that secondary cost was more than $200,000. That money was needed only because we had chosen to provide interior corridors to **connect space**.

In a flash, my VA training took hold. What other way was there to **connect space**? And the answer that hit me was: use a balcony.

I knew that the American Institute of Architects (AIA) measurement standards used by all architects counts balcony areas as worth one-half the gross area given to a building. And in addition, I knew that none of the cost of the **guide egress** secondary function was required for open balconies. Therefore, the worth of the function **connect space** was at least half of what it was costing. The worth of the corridor secondary function shouldn't be more than the worth of a bedroom basic function.

I had in front of me, at the table, a commercial building cost book. I looked up residential buildings with balconies—namely motels—and sure enough, the book said we could build the full square footage of our barracks within our budget if it were built like a motel.

After the captain finished his diatribe about the poor living conditions we were providing—and couldn't even afford that—the other managers threw their hands up at a loss as to what to do. Then I spoke up.

I said, "Captain, if we didn't spend any more money than we had, and if we got 360 people in the building, do you think the Navy would allow us to build a Holiday Inn?"

Somebody at the other end of the table muttered, "Holiday Inn. Hell, that would be too good for them!"

At that moment the captain leaped to his feet and said, "That's exactly what we should build. Why, every room has a toilet!"

He ordered me to get with the branch manager of architecture, work out a concept, and validate the budget to build a barracks with a balcony. In so doing, we realized that a corridor does have a few other secondary functions that were necessary to take care of in our concept.

We needed corridors to **connect rooms**—the bedroom with the bathroom, the lounge, and the laundry equipment—so the corpsman could go around in his T-shirt before having to fully dress to go outside.

The solution, as seen here, was to make a six-bedroom module with a very short corridor so that no room was more than three feet from the toilet room door or six feet from the lounge. This exceeded the captain's dream!

The design resulted in a three-story building with five modules per floor as shown. The compactness of each module resulted in unexpected savings in fan coil unit HVAC distribution, electrical wiring, and structural cost.

It resulted in a very high-quality building in terms of its space, amenities, and livability compared with the barracks concepts of old. The National Capital Planning Commission strongly endorsed this new design by stating in part, "The Commission commends the Department of the Navy for developing a promising new concept in barracks design. The proposed 24-man module eliminates the need for long corridors and provides a large lounge, which gives each module an intimate scale. The Commission feels that this concept will greatly improve the institutional character typical of most military barracks."

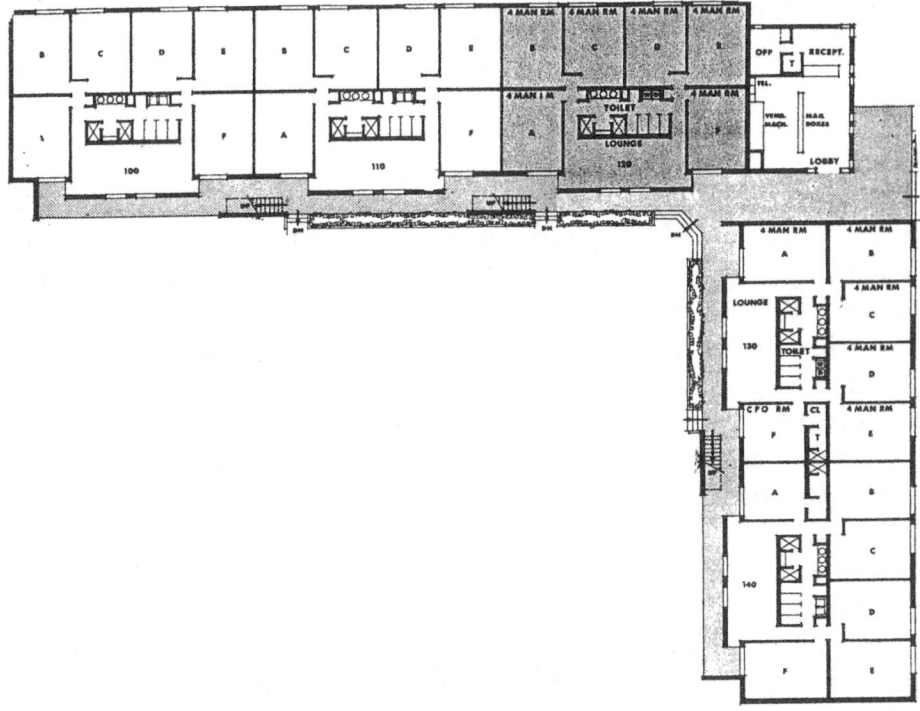

Value analysis (function-inspired change) works. It got the Navy corpsman the better housing it needed within the budget.

It also worked again when the U.S. Coast Guard approached us that same year to help redesign their enlisted quarters on Governor's Island in New York. The Coast Guard had failed to design within their budget for three years and were about to lose their funding. The new concept helped save the day.

Next we successfully applied our concept to the design of a new Marine Corps barracks for Quantico. We were the only Navy Field Division that didn't need to ask for more money to produce enlisted quarters. Following this, we were asked by Department of Defense (DoD) to develop a tri-service design standard for the Army, Navy, and Air Force—all based on the open-balcony concept.

It is more than forty-five years later, and the enlisted modular suite concept at Bethesda, Maryland, still stands. It was recently converted to quarters for families visiting the hospital. A successful reuse that would have been much more difficult using the old, center-hall barracks design.

***

Three years later I was promoted to Deputy Director of value analysis for the U.S. Naval Air System Command (NAVAIR) in Washington, D.C. As a new person to the organization, I asked to see the accounting expenditure data for all field naval rework facilities under the command. I could then better understand what they did, what they spent, where the areas of highest cost were, and where to focus our VA effort.

I came across one field rework maintenance facility that had been purchasing screwdrivers repeatedly by the case. We all joked about how much **transmitting torque** they must be doing, but it was still worth looking into during my "get acquainted" field trip.

I quickly discovered that part of the aircraft maintenance procedure was to touch up the paint on the fuselage before releasing the aircraft back to the flight line. The maintenance worker drew paint from supply storage and then a screwdriver from the tool room. He used the screwdriver to **pry lid** and then **stir paint**. Both of these uses became functions of the screwdriver — a function being the purpose for which the user obtains an item.

To make matters worse, they used red, white, and blue enamel paint, which required three screwdrivers so as not to mix the paint colors. Of course when they were all dirty with dried enamel, they were thrown in the dustbin until new ones were needed for maintenance on the next bird.

Needless to say, we put a stop to that by issuing wooden sticks with the paint and saved a few bucks for the taxpayer.

***

As deputy VA manager, the command assigned me to sit on the Configuration Control Board (CCB) that reviewed all changes to aircraft. I soon learned that cockpit configuration was sacred.

They hated to change anything in the cockpit to prevent having confused pilots or the need to retrain them.

One of the key instruments in the cockpit of a fighter aircraft was the Bearing Distance Heading Indicator (BDHI). And just as it sounds, its function was to **display bearing** (angle toward where the pilot wanted to fly) and **display distance** to that location. It worked by receiving a radio signal from the destination using the Tactical Air Navigation (TACAN) system and then displaying the two bits of information.

I learned that the new in-production aircraft of Navy fighter jets from Grumman Aircraft had an onboard Inertial Navigation System (INS) that could calculate for the pilot his exact latitude and longitude at any point as he was flying. As the only civil engineer on NAVAIR's staff, I also knew that if you had the latitude and longitude of where you wanted to go, you could use simple math to calculate the bearing and distance between two points if you knew where you were. I decided to study this issue when I realized from my surveying experience that the two functions of the expensive TACAN system could be achieved in a much more cost-effective manner.

The modern-day fighter aircraft has several onboard computers for its other systems. I postulated that if one could hijack a small amount of space on one of those existing computers, it could feed the BDHI with the bearing and distance between the two points. All a pilot would need is a small keypad to insert the latitude and longitude of his destination to the computer, have the INS send its constant feed to the computer, and read the result on the BDHI. No cockpit configuration change was needed!

I checked with a sister command, the program manager of the Shipboard Inertial Navigation System (SINs) at the Navy Bureau of Ships. He thought it was an excellent, workable idea. He told me something else of vital importance: "TACAN is only a peacetime system. During war, the aircraft carrier turns it off so the enemy cannot detect the radio transmission and reveal the location of the ship. For a fixed-base airport it makes no difference. Everyone knows its latitude and longitude from a map. For carrier operation, we hold preflight meetings and tell the pilots the rendezvous point."

I asked, "How then, does the pilot get back to the ship?"

He replied, "The pilot uses a clipboard in his lap and manually calculates the bearing and distance." He only has to be accurate up to a couple of miles because the aircraft carrier can turn on a local All Weather Carrier Landing System (AWCLS) to guide the aircraft onto the landing deck.

I checked with NAVAIR's testing center and found that it would only cost $20,000 to develop a computer program to test the new concept on the first six birds under production. That was a drop in the bucket compared to the $85,000 TACAN in each aircraft and the extra fifty-five pounds of weight it brought. Reduction of weight in an aircraft was of extreme importance because it meant increased performance — range, speed, and payload.

I was excited that I had an idea from function analysis that really mattered. I had never been in an aircraft or on an aircraft carrier; never seen a BDHI, a TACAN, or an INS. Yet here was an idea with great potential.

I prepared a letter for the commander of NAVAIR to sign off on ordering the test to delete the TACAN System. It was never signed. The unwritten reason cited to me was the handwriting on the wall. It would eliminate 450 field personnel whose dedicated job was to support TACAN.

I told this story to a good friend, Harold G. Tufty, CVS, FSAVE, who said to me, "You just affected someone's rice bowl."

The lesson learned: it is tough to battle politics!

✳✳✳

One of my first duties in my new position at the General Services Administration was to review the budget of the $54 million Consolidated Federal Law Enforcement Training Center under design for Beltsville, Maryland. In looking over the budget I noticed a line item for a guardhouse in the center of the road at the main gate. Its cost was estimated to be $450,000.

One of the notes I made on the submittal package that was sent back to the architect said, "You had better VA the guardhouse."

The prominent Georgetown architect took umbrage with my note and complained to my boss, the commissioner of the Public Buildings Service, Arthur Sampson. The architect didn't know it, but Mr. Sampson liked VA. He was from state government in Pennsylvania and was an Honorary Vice President of SAVE.

I was called into the commissioner's office to face the music. The architect stated, "I haven't even designed the guardhouse yet, and he's trying to screw it up. How does he know what it will cost when I get finished?"

I replied, "I don't know what it will cost but I know **housing guard** isn't worth $450,000.

The architect said, "How do you know that?"

I said, "Because I just bought a five-bedroom home in Virginia for $58,000, and it wasn't even on government land!"

The commissioner grinned and excused me.

I stayed on to monitor the design, and what a monster was created. A small drainage ditch became a river with large-span bridges to cross over to the training building on the other side. The athletic building on this side of the river had a pool, with its shallow end against the bank of the river. I suggested rotating the pool to put the deep end against the river, which would balance the water pressures and reduce cost.

The architect's concept aerial view showed that the river emptied into a lake formed in the woods. I tried to get the architect to tell me the function of the lake, with no success. Was it to **see water**? No, because the trees are in the way and it can't be seen from the buildings. Is it to **feel water**? No, because there is no road or path access to the lake. Is it to **taste water**? No, because the water is not purified. Is it to **hear water**? No, because the water is stagnant. Well, is it to **smell water**? Probably!

At any rate, despite all the available land, the architect placed the tennis courts on the roof of the athletic building. The roof was not only **excluding elements** but was also performing as an open-air floor to support more load than necessary, thereby increasing the cost of the **exclude element** function more than that function was worth. We asked to have the tennis courts relocated to the ground.

When I told the architect of the budgetary problems on the project, the architect said, "Well, my building is within budget."

"That may be true, but the whole project is not," I said.

The Office of Management and Budget ultimately cancelled the whole project because of its cost. They moved the training center to an unused facility at the Naval Air Station at Glynco, Georgia, where it remains today. The taxpayers won this one and so did the State of Georgia.

✳✳✳

As you can see, value analysis works on whole projects and all of their separate components and parts. However, no matter how good the technique, change does not come without executive management support.

CHAPTER 6

Saving the World

For which of you, intending to build a tower, sitteth
not down first, and counteth the cost, whether he have
sufficient to finish it?

- LUKE **14:28**

It can be argued that the basic functions of the United States Federal Government are to establish justice, insure domestic tranquility, provide for common defense, promote general welfare, and secure blessings of liberty by performing requested services at the national level for the collective group—services that those individuals cannot do for themselves at state, local, or individual levels.

Our quest is that world executives would use VA—the proven legacy technique—to solve its problems of management strife, including cost overruns, debt, and deficit.

However, stepping down from the world to the level of a federal agency or a major corporation is the highest level VA has been permitted to operate to "do its thing."

All organizations have mission creep and confusion, which divert resources from their main objective.

***

This is the story of one major legacy federal entity[10] that has been around since its creation by Congress in 1779. Each U.S. Army Corps of Engineers (USACE) leader does a good job of tracking his or her respective, assigned missions, which have grown in complexity over 200 years. However, it is truly difficult for any leader to comprehend how ALL missions interact, as well as ALL applicable, interacting laws.

VA has been used for decades as a tool for resolving problems and better stating the value of an organization. Value workshops serve as a tool to better tell the USACE story.

Value workshops offer the potential to elicit the innovation necessary and help grow the culture into a "learning organization.[11]" Learning organizations are self-renewing organizations, which practice five key disciplines. It so happens that those five disciplines are also practiced during execution of the value job plan.[12] They include:

- Shared understanding
- Shared vision
- Systems/team thinking
- Mental models
- Personal mastery

Using value study workshops to enable results-oriented, creative collaboration is instrumental in any change initiative underway in an organization.

---

10 Sponsor: U.S. Army Corps of Engineers (USACE), VA workshop led by: Michael P. Holt, PE, CVS.

11 'Learning organization' is a management concept popularized in the 1980s through Peter Senge's Fifth Discipline.

12 Value Job Plan consists of the following study phases: Information, Function, Creative, Evaluation, Development, Presentation, and Implementation.

***

A high-level headquarters meeting was held to offer input to a Department of Defense (DoD) discussion. The DoD seemed to be on a decision path that had the potential to eliminate USACE from participating in one of its programs, and to damage potential USACE participation in Homeland Security efforts. The DoD was pursuing assistance on four fronts:

- Solving domestic issues
- Solving economic issues
- Solving national security issues
- Providing homeland security

The meeting group was struggling to convey what the Corps offered to its customers. "We are the nation's engineers," was one of the responses offered during the first hour of verbal interchange. "They NEED us," came another, offered at the same time someone else was speaking. Each of the leaders in the room was certain that DoD simply had to include his or her particular discipline in future work.

The USACE headquarters group had heard nothing that might be construed as excluding, replacing, or minimizing the responsibilities of the Corps. Yet the same group was struggling somewhat to define those responsibilities.

The VA manager accepted the challenge to help the group prepare a series of function diagrams (FAST)[13]. The diagrams were intended to show how USACE expertise might be critical to the DoD functions under discussion.

The group spent about fifteen minutes offering as many USACE functions of which they were aware. The VA manager and an attorney in the group spent the next few weeks associating laws with these functions and creating three function diagrams.

---

13 Function Analysis System Technique (FAST) diagrams, invented by Charles Bytheway to display function logic.

Many functions changed after reviewing the actual laws, and many were added. Many were dropped in order to only show the functions for which the USACE had direct authority. The Corps had significant capabilities, but many functions were only performed when another agency requested and funded such function.

It was further discovered that in placement on a FAST diagram, it did not matter if the functions' verbs/nouns come from law, mission, or circular—legal hierarchy did not matter. It further did not matter at what point in time a direction occurred. One still had to place functions in HOW/WHY order. Sometimes a recent directive was right beside an older directive. All situations were acceptable.

First, for everyday peacetime, the Corps headquarters group identified the following three basic functions that USACE could contribute to three of the four stated needs of the DoD:

- **Manage water resources**
    Navigation
    Flood damage reduction
    Hydropower
    Municipal/industrial water storage
- **Develop DoD facilities** (army and air force)
- **Construct/Operate campsites** (at lakes)

These basic—and many secondary—functions could certainly contribute to the fourth needed function, **providing homeland security**, yet there was no legal authority for such a function during peacetime, unless requested by another agency. The following is a sample FAST diagram for the everyday direct authority of the Army Corps of Engineers.

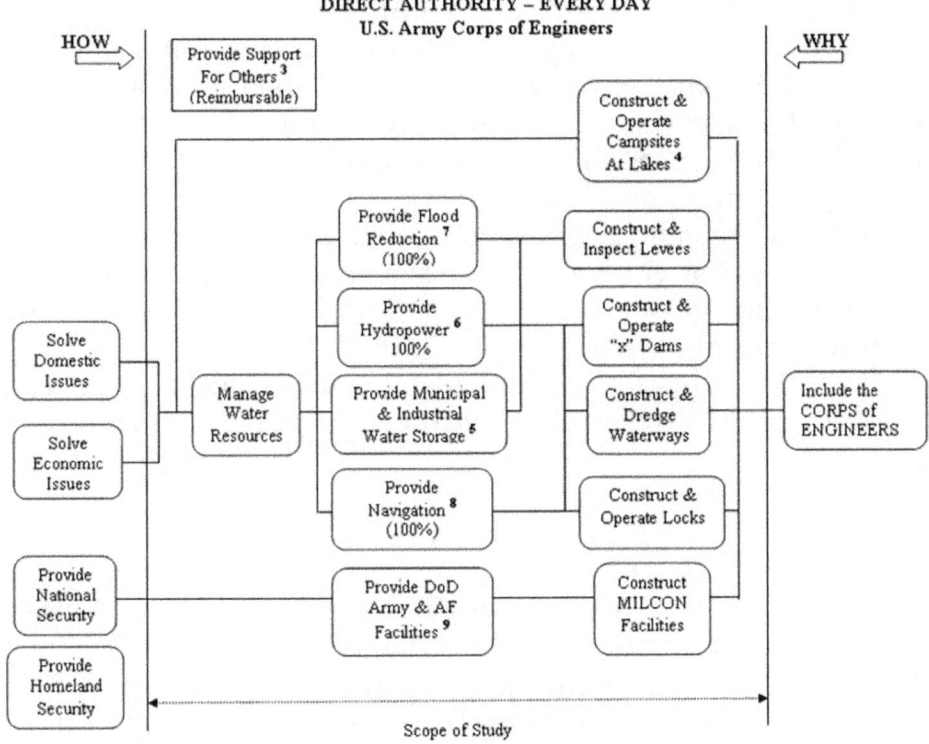

Associated with each function in the above diagram is the pertinent law that provides for the function. A partial list for example is:

3 10 United States Code (USC) 3036(d)(2);
    31 USC 1535;   33 USC 2323a;   22USC 2357;   33 USC 2314a;
    31 USC 6505;   33 USC 560;   33 USC 701h;   15 USC 3710a,
4 33 USC 460d.
5 43 USC 390b;   33 USC 708.
6 33 USC 825s.
7 33 USC 701a-1;   33 USC 701b.
8 33 USC 540;   33 USC 414;   33 USC 603a; 33 USC 3

During natural disasters, the same basic functions listed above are still provided; however, two additional authorities are added. The Stafford Act offered another "all-the-time" function to assist FEMA on a requested and reimbursable basis, and USACE would then have authority to provide emergency municipal and industrial drinking water. A second FAST diagram was created to show the agency's direct authority during a natural disaster, but USACE still needed requests from others to directly contribute to **providing homeland security**.

A third function diagram was created for national emergencies, and this one contained a significant, basic function that the first two did not—direct authority for USACE to **redistribute civil work funds**.

This third diagram identified a USACE function that can directly link USACE to **providing homeland security** with funding.

***

Since the USACE exercise, function analysis has been used to explain environmental requirements during multi-agency partnering meetings; it has helped leaders of a new army office better understand their directed tasks; and it has been used to help two separate DoD entities find common missions for partnership.

The technique requires significantly more preparation time but offers great value to high-level VA workshops.

The three FAST diagrams were completed and presented to the HQ group at a final meeting. The attending senior executive happily and excitedly interrupted the presentation after less than ten minutes.

She walked to the screen and directed movement of some functions within the diagrams. She then directed that copies of the revised documents be furnished immediately following the meeting. She stated that she needed no more explanation. These diagrams succinctly offered all the knowledge needed for multiple issues occurring within headquarters.

The group now had a functional plan with which to proceed with any response to DoD. Any member of USACE could review these diagrams and have a better understanding of the Corps' abilities. The diagrams are used at headquarters to remind leaders HOW/WHY, when, and even if, many things are done.

During the exercise it was realized that **provide navigation** may be the only function that is solely given to USACE directly by law. That turned out to be the reason that any entity might be required to include USACE in any future work. The Corps, of course, coordinates with the Coast Guard (a Homeland Security Agency), but United States navigation responsibility rests solely with the U.S. Army Corps of Engineers.

A second Ah-ha! moment was the discovery that only USACE, has direct authority to support Homeland Security through the redistribution of Civil Works Program Funds during a national emergency. The Corps had many ways of offering homeland security assistance, but most required requests and funding from others.

Creating these mission function diagrams was exhaustive work, but support the relationship between USACE, DHS, and others.

Suffice it to say, it would do the same for any company with many diverse units, divisions, and outlying entities.

CHAPTER 7

What are People Doing?

Don't talk to the people until you've listened to the people.

- ANN KLEIN, UNITED STATES POLITICIAN

Which strategy is better in times of financial need — slash all budgets by 10 percent or apply VA to identify and study those specific areas where efficiencies can be gained to save the day?

The following comes from a paper written by William L. Kelly.[14]

"In order to achieve the highest and best use of people, management constructs organization charts that define responsibilities and their relationships to maximize efficient production within an organization. However, organization charts become distorted by characteristics of individuals. Therefore, effectiveness and efficiency need periodic checks and adjustments to

---

14 Kelly is a registered PE, a certified value specialist (CVS), and a Fellow of SAVE International.

counter human variables and faulty procedural and systemic elements.

A value study concerning people examines some human characteristics and quirks that distort structured planning. VA provides a method to assess how well organization procedures and processes perform in their presence. An audit system must readily determine deviation from intended actions to expose areas requiring correction. Function Analysis, FAST Diagramming and Linear Responsibility Charting combine to form a prime tool for such analysis and cure."

***

Organization charts are wonderful myths. They intend to distribute authority, responsibility, tasks, and relationship of units; however, they get sabotaged by human idiosyncrasies.

Organization charts expand into standards, rules, flow charts, job descriptions, and process details all bound into procedural manuals. Eventually excessive regulation and oversight suffocate productivity, and need periodic surgery to keep them healthy and competitive.

For example, one value study on a contracting process required seventeen signatures from people in separate offices to approve each change order request. Adding normal diversions like vacations or illness, it often took weeks to obtain all necessary signatures. Signers compounded delay by demanding instant response to their comments, causing mini-approval cycles that continued until all reviewers were satisfied. Organization response to needed changes such as this equaled that of a snail's pace on a sightseeing tour.

Realistic organization charts evolve as you learn who produces, who is trustworthy, who works well with others, and who is knowledgeable and prompt. Shortcuts to those folks establish true lines of interaction and form a working organization chart — the "go to" group system.

Most people want to succeed but their definition of success varies greatly. Some want a paycheck, some just want to get by, others hunger for power, and many want to grow and be productive.

Motivation only comes from one's self. Pleas and pressures to motivate usually produce theater. Five people per hundred will not work even under threat. They left their motivation in the womb. Another 5 percent are self-driven to excel. In between, effort varies from barely acceptable to constant high performance.

People who have time to waste prefer to spend it with those who don't. They bask in the glow of productive enterprise and the results of entrepreneurial people, but without sweating. They dampen productivity and foster resentment.

Ringelmann, a German scientist, had workers pull against a meter (scale) in units of one, two, three, and eight people. Measurements showed the average force generated ranged from 63 kg (139 lbs) for one, 53 kg (117 lbs) for three, and 31 kg (68 lbs) for eight persons. Study results prompted this conclusion: individual effort, on average, contracts relative to the number of people assigned to complete a task.

Mentally unemployed staff continually test how low an effort other members will tolerate and still permit them to remain in a unit or team. Highly motivated people relish learning, solving problems, and producing quality answers. They seek those of like characteristics and tend to ignore, run over, or ostracize those dead in the water.

These and other human characteristics distort all plans whether structuring an organization, process, or individual work unit. Producers must be identified in any reorganization effort.

✳✳✳

How does one diagnose an organization's health, effectiveness, and efficiency, and decide if it is doing the right things and doing the right things right? First, clearly identify problem areas.

Problems can be very large, for example: reorganizing the entire company due to loss or gain of major contracts, acquisition of another firm, or a bureaucratic agency in a quagmire. They can be process-specific like design, quality control, contract administration, production, paperwork, over-regulation, or estimating. Or they can be special cases such as elimination of bottlenecks or to halt empire building. Answers point to wrong priorities, excess or lack of supervision, cronyism, and nepotism. To solve those or similar problems requires complete factual knowledge of "Who Does What."

Headquarters is responsible for organization mission, goals, objectives, and vision. Division and subdivision managers are responsible for translating those big-picture items into specific areas of activity, configuring resources to satisfy them, and managing to ensure success. Staff is responsible for tailoring activities into tasks and matching an individual's abilities to complete those activities and tasks.

The following process brings order, objectivity, and simplicity for diagnosis and restoration of organization health. The VA study example I am using involves combining twenty-two separate agencies into one agency—Homeland Security[15]. The basic functions of the new agency as determined by the VA team were:

- **Restrict enemy**   - **Administer justice**
- **Disrupt terrorism** - **Outperform enemy**
- **Direct activities** - **Minimize impact**
- **Neutralize enemy**

---

15 Sponsor: Department of Homeland Security, Value study conducted by: William L. Kelley, PE, CVS.

FIRST PHASE OF PROCESS FOR 22 AGENCIES X-AXIS = HOMELAND SECURITY DEPARTMENT FUNCTIONS Y AXIS = HEADQUARTERS PLUS ALL AGENCIES	HEADQUARTERS	IMMIGRATION AND NATURALIZATION SER	CUSTOMS SERVICE	ANIMAL AND PLANT HEALTH INSPECTION.	COAST GUARD	FEDERAL PROTECTIVE SERVICE	TRANSPORTATION SECURITY SYSTEM	FEDERAL EMERGENCY MGMT. SYSTEM	CHEMICAL, BIOLOGICAL, RADIOLOGICAL AND NUCLEAR RESPONSE ASSETS	DOMESTIC EMERGENCY SUPPORT TEAM	NUCLEAR INCIDENT RESPONSE	OFFICE OF DOMESTIC PREPAREDNESS	NATL DOMESTIC PREP. OFFICE	CIVILIAN BIO-DEFENSE RESEARCH PROG	ET. AL
HIGHER ORDER FUNCTION															
OVERCOME TERRORISM															
BASIC FUNCTIONS		PRESIDENT, VP AND CFO OR EQUIVALENT LEVEL LEADERS TAKE PART IN THIS PHASE													
RESTRICT ENEMY															
ADMINISTER JUSTICE		BUILD THE SKELETON'S BACKBONE.													
DISRUPT TERRORISM		1. WHO IS RESPONSIBLE FOR EACH FUNCTION?													
OUTPERFORM ENEMY		2. IF MORE THAN ONE GROUP CLAIMS IT,													
DIRECT ACTIVITIES		DETERMINE WEIGHT OF EVIDENCE AS PERCENT													
MINIMIZE IMPACT		AND SELECT THE BEST QUALIFIED OWNER.													
NEUTRALIZE ENEMY		3. THE BUCK MUST STOP IN ONE PLACE.													
		4. TO SUBLET RESPONSIBILITY TO OTHER													
		AGENCIES DOES NOT TAKE THE MONKEY OFF THE													
		OWNER'S BACK.													

Mission, goals, and objectives were converted into a group of thirty to forty functions sufficient to begin understanding the new organization. Following this, the study was broken down into three phases through the preparation of linear charts.

SECOND PHASE OF PROCESS INCLUDES ALL 22 AGENCIES ANALYZED SEPARATELY X-AXIS = BASIC PLUS MAJOR SECONDARY FUNCTIONS Y AXIS = 22 AGENCIES (ON SEPARATE FORMS)	IMMIGRATION AND NATR. SERVICE	CUSTOMS SERVICE	ANIMAL AND PLANT HEALTH INSPEC.	COAST GUARD	FEDERAL PROTECTIVE SERVICE	TRANSPORTATION SECURITY SYSTEM	FEDERAL EMER. MGMT. SYSTEM	CHEM, BIOLOG, RAD AND NUC RESP	DOMESTIC EMERGENCY.SUPP TEAM	NUCLEAR INCIDENT RESPONSE	OFFICE OF DOMESTIC PREPAREDNESS	NATL DOMESTIC PREP. OFFICE	CIVILIAN BIODEFENCE RESEARCH PRO	LAWRENCE LIVERMORE NATL LAB	ET.AL.
BASIC FUNCTION RESTRICT ENEMY															
SECONDARY FUNCTIONS SECURE BORDERS PROHIBIT MOVEMENT EXCLUDE UNDESIRABLES NETWORK ENFORCERS	DEPARTMENT, BRANCH AND SECTION HEADS FURNISH INPUT FOR THESE DETERMINATIONS. INTERVIEWERS LEAD ALL EFFORTS.														
BASIC FUNCTION ADMINISTER JUSTICE															
SECONDARY FUNCTIONS ENFORCE LAWS PRESERVE RIGHTS	COMPLETE THE SKELETON'S FORM. 1. WHAT COMPONENTS ARE BEST EQUIPPED TO SATISFY EACH SECONDARY FUNCTION?														
BASIC FUNCTION DISRUPT TERRORISM	2. THEY WILL COMPETE FOR OWNERSHIP. THOSE WITH ZERO OR VERY LITTLE EXPERTISE WILL DROP OUT TO SIMPLIFY THE SELECTION PROCESS. ONE COMPONENT WILL BE NAMED OWNER FOR EACH SECONDARY FUNCTION.														
SECONDARY FUNCTIONS CAPTURE CRIMINALS PURSUE TERRORISTS ESTABLISH PARTNERSHIPS ESTAB UNDERGROUND ELIMINATE HIDEOUTS DENY SUPPORT CAPTURE ASSETS NEUTRALIZE SUPPLIERS	3. UNPICKED COMPONENTS WILL REMAIN WITH THEIR AGENCY. IT MAY BE REORGANIZED, DISBANDED OR ABSORBED BY ANOTHER AGENCY. FOR EXAMPLE, FEMA WILL SPLIT. NATURE-CAUSED DISASTERS ADDRESSED OUTSIDE DHS AND HUMAN INDUCED DISASTERS INSIDE DHS. THAT KIND OF SPLIT MUST BE DETERMINED FOR ALL 22 AGENCIES.														

Highest-level charts show responsibility for managing the organization and major activities (higher order and basic functions). Higher order and basic functions are placed on the x-axis. Headquarters and major divisions are atop columns on the y-axis. President, vice president, CFO, or equivalent positions can follow major divisions.

Phase II are mid-level charts that identify subdivisions responsible for managing secondary-function-level activities. Each basic function is subdivided into secondary functions that become listed on the x-axis in descending level of indenture. Organization subdivisions can be followed by their manager, assistants, and top supervisors listed atop y-axis columns.

Phase III breaks this down further. Each secondary function from Phase II is broken into individual tasks, which are listed on the x-axis in descending level of indenture. Job titles top the y-axis columns.

Phase III shows individual contribution to each task and the form it takes. Charts display individual duties, types of participation, and relationships.

***

This type of function analysis is somewhat tedious and detailed, but the results can be astounding. One can tell if responsibility is rightly claimed, claimed by an unintended unit or executive, overlaps others, is not claimed at all, or is shared with other units as a percentage of involvement.

Chart information can be processed to show multitudes of critical data, including: essential tasks and services required for specific functions or projects; duties broken down by type—executive, supervisory, administrative, or worker; duplication, overlap, underserved, needless, overworked, and other faults are exposed. Duties of a specific unit or person are summarized.

The ideal firm is one person; second best is two partners. As firms grow, personal responsibility and accountability diminish, substituted by finger pointing. All governments prove excessive staff survives on mediocrity through anonymity. So do bloated private organizations.

Start anew. Verify or establish a clear mission, goals, and objectives. Convert those to higher order and basic functions, then expand to construct a complete picture of the organization. Settle which main divisions are responsible for higher order and each basic function. Follow that by determining which subdivisions own secondary functions. Last, convert basic and secondary functions to tasks, interview candidates, and select the most qualified people to perform them.

Ask this question of every function or task: Is this best done in-house or outsourced?

Practice makes perfect. The VA process helps to diagnose and cure organizations and their problems. It brings simplicity, objectivity, and discipline to the process.

CHAPTER 8

To Consolidate or Not

It's amazing what people can do if they set out without
preconceived notions.

- BEN STEIN

The study in this example started out with the preconceived
notion that consolidating two units into one would be cheaper.
We can't blame management for that. They did their job in
identifying the issue and asking for the VA study.

Companies and agencies with multiple offices in multiple cities
performing similar functions are ripe for a VA study. The worth
of redundant functions is always suspect and subject to analysis.

As a result, the VA team was charged by management with
answering seven questions as part of their review.

- Should they maintain split programs at both locations for
the same sponsor?

- Should they maintain a separate photography group, editing group, publishing group, and website for each?
- Should each program have a director at each center?
- Should there be two separate centers?
- Does the current program serve the agency needs?
- What are some alternative functional and operational models that would improve the business processes of the program?
- Are there cost savings opportunities?

Here is the case history[16] in question.

A large, government agency had two research centers at different locations and wanted to explore their operations for value improvement. Each center had separate directors, staffs, budgets, publications groups, websites, and program workload. This value study included an analysis of organizational structure, staffing, work distribution, communication, websites (style, templates, management, etc.), project submittal acceptance, overhead structure and costs, business processes, and overall national governance.

The study also included review of center management, supervision, direction, location, operational directives, administrative and publishing integration, and other related functions.

A three-day, pre-study, information-phase value workshop was held at each of the two center locations with a team of employees to determine the functions being performed at each location.

The space area occupied by both centers was obtained:

---

16 Sponsor: Kurt Gernerd, Assistant Director, Engineering, U.S. Forest Service, Study led by: Stephen Kirk, PhD, FAIA, FSAVE, CVS-Life, LEED AP, Kirk Associates, LLC.

Area	SF
Main Entrance	237
Conference Center	3,427
Main Floor	15,952
Second Floor	15,952
Textile Lab	7,481
Model 52	-
Storage	2,418
Fabrication Shops	17,642
Total	63,109

Program cost components were listed in the following format for each center:

Program/Cost Components	Qty	Unit	Net Cost	Sub-Total	Total
Reforestation					418,000
Labor	1	FTE	100,000	400,000	
State & Private	1	LS	18,000	18,000	
Travel	1	LS	0	0	
Materials	1	LS	0	0	
Safety & Health					100,000
Labor	1	FTE	100,000	100,000	
State & Private	1	LS	0	0	
Travel	1	LS	0	0	
Materials	1	LS	0	0	
Engineering					2,750,000
Labor	25	FTE	100,000	2,500,000	
Misc.	1	LS	250,000	250,000	
Contract Consult.	1	LS	0	0	
Travel	1	LS	0	0	
Private Contracts	1	LS	0	0	
Publications	1	LS	0	0	
Etc.					

Life-cycle costs were computed for both centers, as shown below, based on a 25-year life span and the federal Office of Management & Budget (OMB) 7% discount rate.

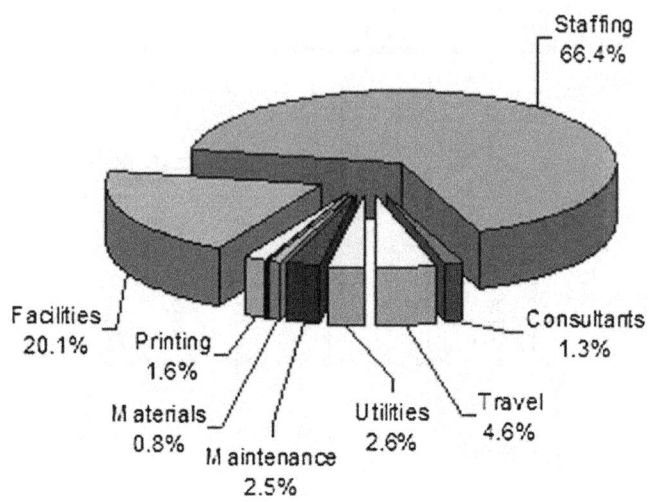

An analysis of the funding received by each center was made and titled Sponsor Support. This helped the VA team and management visualize the sources, the amount of funding being provided, and the cost per employee at each center of operation.

Sponsor Support

	Current		Center 1	Center 2
Fire & Aviation Mgmt	3,500,000		1,750,000	1,750,000
Engineering	2,200,000		400,000	1,200,000
Recreation	1,000,000		500,000	500,000
Forest Mgmt & Nurseries	800,000		0	200,000
Occ. Safety & Health	400,000		400,000	0
Watershed Soil & Air	250,000		65,000	185,000
Chief Information Office	250,000		250,000	0
Forest Health & Protection	170,000		170,000	0
Total	$8,570,000		$3,535,000	$5,085,000
	Employees		42	44
	Cost/Employee		$84,157	$114,432

A Pareto chart was developed to help visualize where a minority of the centers' programs spend a majority of the sponsor's funding.

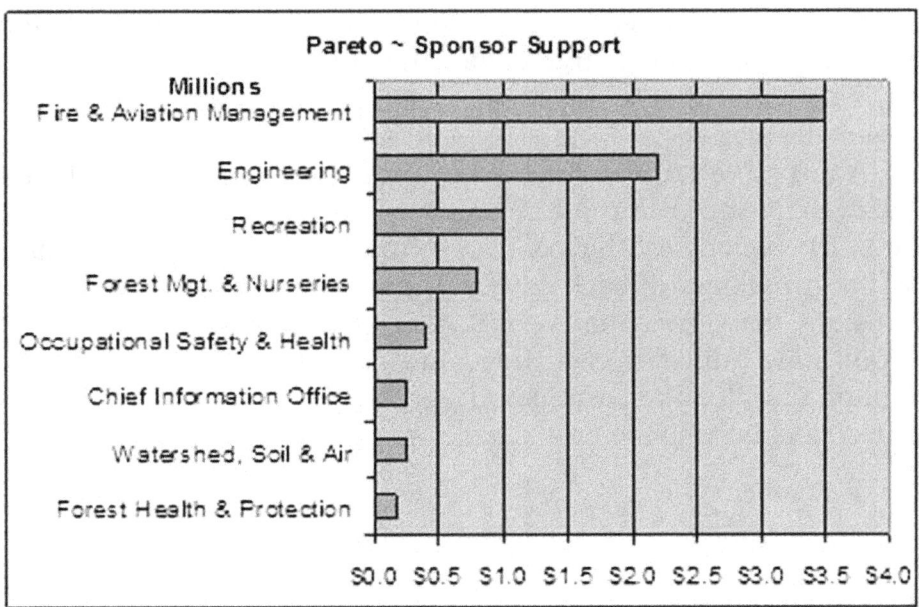

Pareto ~ Sponsor Support

Combining all of the individual program functions and costs for both centers led to the identification of two major functions out of the seven basic functions that seemed best candidates for value improvement. These were the **transfer technology** and **develop product** functions. These two were costing $3.2 and $2.6 million respectively out of the agency's $10.2 million budget.

One function management requested the value study explore was how to **consolidate resources** to **transfer technology** and **develop products** while maintaining effectiveness. This led to the ideation of the following seven alternatives:

- Alt 1   Two centers under two programs (original condition)
- Alt 1A Two separate centers under one program
- Alt 2   One center: Center 1 is turned over to Center 2
- Alt 2A One center: Center 1 property given to Agency "x"
- Alt 3   One center: Center 2 is turned over to Center 1
- Alt 4   One center in new location: Center 1 property transferred to Agency "x" and Center 2 property transferred to Agency "z"
- Alt 4A One center in new location: both properties transferred to Agency "y" or sold

An intense choosing-by-advantages (CBA)[17] analysis of the benefits of each alternative versus the life-cycle cost of each alternative produced the following graphic displaying the above seven alternatives.

Alternative 1A was selected for implementation at a reduced life-cycle cost of $15 million because it preserved and enhanced all of the benefits of the existing solution. The agency now has a staffing manager at each center. It has one center manager, one assistant manager, one website, one photo group, one budget group, one publications group, and one program leader per $1 million workload to handle both centers. One program operating in two locations is the new theme.

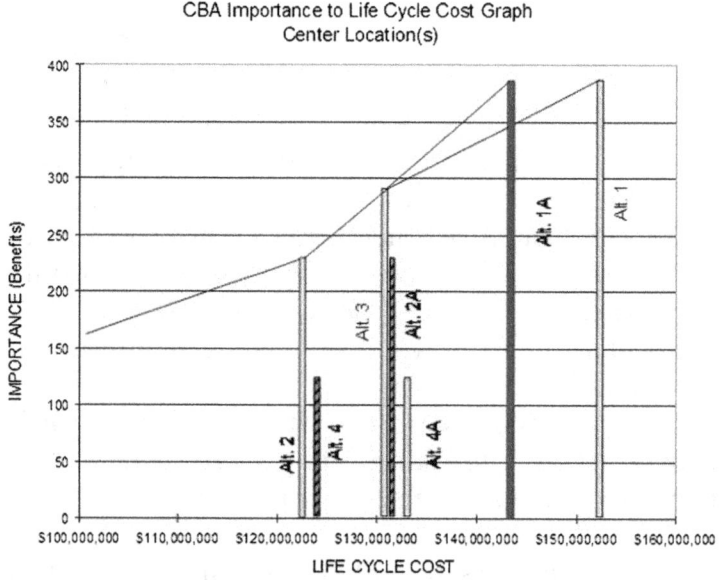

CBA Importance to Life Cycle Cost Graph
Center Location(s)

The above is just one example from a 120-page study report for the organization that resulted in 211 ideas for value enhancement. Of these, eleven proposals were formally presented to management, which produced forty-seven performance benefits:

---

17 CHOOSING BY ADVANTAGES® (CBA) developed by Jim Suhr, The Institute for Decision Innovations, Inc.

Performance Benefits	Proposals
Improved field support	6
Operational effectiveness/efficiency	10
Standardization	4
Flexibility	6
Improved synergy	5
Improved image	8
Other	<u>8</u>
	47

Other benefits included: improved leadership, personnel savings, increased revenue, improved technology transfer, and improved morale from being involved in nationally significant projects. It also built the capability to meet future staffing needs and improved productivity of technical staff. It better addressed one-time, short-term specialist needs, stability of the application research program, and expanded utilization of agreements and authorities with related initial-cost savings and life-cycle–cost savings.

CHAPTER 9

Enhancing Revenue

A man who pays his bills on time is soon forgotten.

- Oscar Wilde

Everyone wants more profit and cash flow. And those who bill others want to be paid.

Companies that charge others for their products, and those agencies that charge others for their services to support their budgets, need to read this one.

Normally there are only three ways to increase revenue — increase prices, reduce costs, or improve sales (make it up in volume). Each of these three methods has their own pitfalls, which I won't take the time to discuss here.

However in the example shown below, VA offered a fourth way — improve the efficiency and effectiveness of collecting what is owed.

***

A major hospital system[18] was having revenue challenges and requested that a value study be conducted to ensure they were getting paid appropriately for all services rendered. Areas studied during the workshops included registration, admitting, billing, finance, insurance counseling, IT systems, as well as physicians' and nurses' services that impacted revenues.

They knew that when discussing the current process, it was important to have the intended functions serve as the baseline for analysis, rather than the activities or processes that make up that function.

Functions served as the best baseline for evaluation because there are often multiple means of providing the same function, whereas the alternatives for a specific activity or process may be much more limited.

For instance, when considering the hospital revenue-impacting function of **register patient**, many alternatives could serve the purpose of registering—either electronically or written, by interview or by completing a form, or any combination of these. Thus, **register patient** was the proper function to analyze in baseline discussions of the current revenue processes. Conversely, the activity of "input patient information into software" is very specific, and would limit potential alternatives for this portion of the revenue process.

Flowcharts were used to generate very detailed descriptions of the current, specific activities taking place to fulfill each function.

Next, the team developed a function diagram to cover the **register patient** function, connecting with the **collect revenue** function and all the intervening functions, to reach the overall goal of **enhancing revenue**.

Because of the abbreviated nature of a VA study it is important to identify the key areas within the processes or hospital where improvements would provide the greatest revenue benefit. The tool used in this study was "Pareto's Law of Maldistribution," otherwise known as the "80/20 Rule."

---

18 Sponsor: Jill Woller, CVS-Life, FSAVE—VE Program Director, New York City, Office of Management and Budget, Study led by: Tom Orr, PE, CVS and Wade Martin, CCC, CVS—U.S. Cost, Inc.

In taking a function-based approach to Pareto's Law, the value study process seeks to identify the 20% of the revenue functions or hospital departments that account for 80% of the revenue capture. The majority of time in the creative-idea session of the study is then focused on improvement alternatives in these key revenue-generating functions or departments. In healthcare, the primary revenue-generating functions include some combination of the following:

- Registration/Patient insurance information
- Admissions
- Coding/Charge capture
- Billing
- Cashier

A similar approach was taken in identifying the 20% of the hospital's departments that generate 80% of the revenues. The workshop focused on generating improvement ideas for processes within these key departments.

- Inpatient
- Emergency room
- Surgery
- Top specialty areas

The outcome of the value study, as expected, was successful. It resulted in 125 creative ideas, thirty-eight of which were developed into proposals or initiatives. From there, thirty-five proposals were accepted, with a projected revenue capture of $17,712,000. Some of the accepted revenue-enhancing initiatives included the following:

- Hire additional personnel in training unit, utilization management, coding, billing, and accounts receivable
- Provide additional office equipment in key revenue departments

- Establish and evaluate performance standards for staff positions
- Construct office space for a consolidated billing department
- Re-bill all outstanding outpatient claims
- Increase communication with payers to reduce front-end denials
- Incorporate patient-information–verification tools and conduct training
- Train doctors, nurses, and coders on standards for appropriate reimbursement
- Train registration staff on how to query patients and enter information in systems
- Upgrade salary of specific positions to attract and retain qualified personnel

The hospital acknowledged that implementing the thirty-five new initiatives concurrently would not be feasible, thus they decided to separate the implementation into three phases.

Twelve initiatives were selected for execution in Phase I, which required a ten-month implementation period. A total of six interdepartmental committees were established to implement these initiatives.

During the workshop, it was estimated that $7,679,000 in additional revenue would be achieved through implementation of the first twelve initiatives. The results, tracked over the ten-month period, identified $6,210,000 in new revenues generated from these initiatives, or approximately 81% of the study estimates. Expenditures of $1,459,000 were spent on Phase I, with over half of the costs attributed to construction of new office space for the outpatient billing department. The remaining expenses were primarily spent on hiring personnel in short-staffed, revenue-generating positions.

When initiatives in Phases II and III are fully implemented — if the actual revenues collected are projected at 80% of workshop estimates — the value study results are projected as follows:

Phase	*Cost	*Estimated Revenue	*Actual Collections
I – Actual	$1,459	$7,679	$6,210
II – Potential	$704	$5,865	$4,690
III – Potential	$215	$4,168	$3,335
Potential Totals –	**$2,377**	**$17,712**	**$14,235**

*all amounts are in 1,000s
**based on Phase I experience: 81% of Estimated Revenue

In addition to the revenue improvements tracked in the Phase I implementation period, the following benefits have also been attributed to the VA initiatives:

- Reduced final denials by 41% from prior year
- Reduced initial-denial rate from 12% down to 2%
- Reduced length of stay
- Much improved accuracy of accounts receivable
- Strengthened ability to negotiate with managed-care payers on denials and outstanding payments
- Improved patient satisfaction, fewer complaints
- Improved employee morale
- Common location of revenue departments allow for long-term increase in revenue capture
- Reduced return mail by 53% over prior year due to improved patient information capture
- Reduced postage costs by $105,000 a year
- Increased revenue by converting self-pay to other insurance options (up 58%)
- More timely and accurate billing
- Improved demographic and financial-data collection

Once the collections are realized for all three phases of the VA initiatives shown above, the return on investment (ROI) of the additional revenue compared to the cost of the value study workshop are expected to exceed 100:1.

***

The sponsor of this study said, "I do think that part of VA's power is the efficiency of the value methodology compared to other management tools, which can take months just to offer meaningful suggestions. In a five-day value workshop, more can be done to jump-start a change effort than using any other technique."

The city now has a hospital staff that is responsible for the workflow, generated the ideas—and through the workshop, gained a new big-picture mindset and a new role of internal-change agent. They also found common ground with others in different departments, which will ease implementation. This improved communication and reduced resistance to change is no small thing for an organization.

CHAPTER 10

Time is Money

If time be of all things the most precious, wasting time
must be the greatest prodigality.

- BENJAMIN FRANKLIN

Not every measure of cost and worth for a VA study is measured in dollars and cents. Time — minutes, workforce hours, and workforce days — are also resources of value.

The problem is, most managers don't really know what time is spent doing work in their organization when work becomes so routine coming in and out of the door.

I was with an organization that processed Standard Form 81 (SF-81) of the federal government, which is a request for space. I asked the top man how much it cost to process each request for space. His answer was, "I don't know. I get three thousand of these a year and I have thirty-seven people on my staff handling those requests and everything else."

Well, I expected that. I wonder if the IRS knows how much it costs them to process their SF-1040s each year. I doubt it. Most companies and agencies don't have budget line items for the functional work they do. They do not keep their accounting information in that fashion.

***

The first requirement, when performing a value study of an existing system, is to make a cost estimate of the existing system.

To estimate the labor cost expended for an existing system in an organization, one needs to find out all the tasks that are being performed, who is performing each task, how long each task takes, the hourly labor rate for the individual performing the task, and the overhead rate for the organization.

The recommended way of estimating labor cost is to develop a flow chart that tracks each operation of system output as it flows through the organization.

And once you have your estimate of the existing system, show it to your boss and get it approved before you start the VA study. If he or she doesn't think the cost is accurate and realistic, they won't believe the outcome of the VA study.

***

My experience was with a processing system to package flat-sheet postage stamps into cartons[19] for delivery to post offices around the country. I led an employee team consisting of a distributor, bookbinder, examiner, packer, and stock controller — all involved in putting the sheets in the cartons.

During the information phase it was determined that they produced 314 cartons of postage stamps per day. There were 400 stamps on each sheet. Quartering them at the post office at the time of sale would produce a hundred stamps per sheet. Each carton held 250,000 stamps, and they produced 59,000 cartons per year.

---

19 Study conducted by: Donald E. Parker, PE, CCE, CVS, FSAVE for the Bureau of Engraving and Printing.

The flag stamps were printed on large presses in another building and delivered to the packaging room by forklift truck in large rolls about three or four feet in diameter. They were dumped on the floor in a receiving area of the room, ready to be cut into sheets, inspected, stacked, counted, shrink wrapped, boxed, and labeled.

We made a flow chart documenting the time spent daily by each employee for each function they performed in the process to produce the 314 cartons. And with knowledge of their wage rates, determined the following function costs per carton:

Load sheets	$ 0.19
Move product	$ 2.58
Unload sheets	$ 0.50
Inspect sheets	$ 3.87
Handle defects	$ 0.54
Count product	$ 1.70
Cut sheets	$ 0.54
Wrap sheets	$ 0.45
Box product	$ 0.90
Mark product	$ 0.10
Keep records	$ 0.30
	$12.18

In addition to that, an overhead cost per carton was computed, which included:

Supervision	$ 1.20
Materials	$ 3.41 (carton, wrap, tape, label)
Clerical	$ 0.02
Depreciation	$ 1.32 (11% for equipment)
Facility overhead	$10.10 (estimated at 83%)
	$16.07

Therefore, the total cost of one carton ready to go out the door was **$28.25** each.

In line with Pareto's Law of Maldistribution, the team observed that 27% of the process functions amounted to 73% of the process cost. This was broken down as follows:

Move product	21%
Inspect sheets	31%
Count product	14%
Box product	7%

Our Ah-ha! moment came when we realized from all our analysis that the stock controller was keeping records of and counting every stamp that left the room—either in boxes or in spoilage of stamps that did not pass inspection.

Why was this being done? To **prevent theft** of damaged sheets by employees. The only fallacy in this thinking was that they did not know the exact number of stamps that came in the room because they came in, in rolls, and the length of the rolls varied depending on when the printing press stopped. So the number of stamps on each roll varied.

All that money spent unnecessarily trying to prevent employee theft! And when the discarded stamps did leave the room in a bin, they left under armed guard to go to the shredder located elsewhere in the building.

Our obvious recommendation became to count the rolls coming in and count the boxes going out—to determine productivity—but move a shredder into the packaging room to eliminate the need for the guards and the exposure to loose stamps outside the room.

***

Without commenting on the manufactured product itself, after an intensive three-day study, the team developed these value-improvement changes and annual savings:

- Increase the package size to 30,000 sheets rather than 25,000 quarter sheets: save $65,000

- Increase the wrap size to 500s with 100-unit dividers: save $196,000
- Use a 3"x5" packing label: save $104,000
- Use tray-type plastic sandwich rather than a carton package unit: save $188,000
- Use fan folding on wraps less than one hundred: save $62,000
- Use perforated rather than die-cut inspection slots: save $11,000
- Reduce the label size and quantity by 50%: save $19,000.
- Examine, count, and sort quarter sheets with mechanized assistance: save $228,000
- Shred spoilage in the packaging section: save $21,000
- Count sheets only once, record only the finished product: save $140,000

The VA study for this example system resulted in a 34% savings annually of $833,000 and a new cost per carton of $17.76.

***

We also recommended studying vaults and shipping, which represented more than 60% of the full postage-stamp cost. We recommended taking packaging materials out of the overhead cost category so they would be more visible.

In addition, we mentioned that automating the packaging process could save more than $1 million a year. However, major expenditures for implementing proposed VA actions should not be presented as a lump-sum aggregate, but rather as a sequence of minimum-risk increments.

A manager may be reluctant to risk a total investment against a total return, but may be willing to chance the first phase of an investment sequence.

An important strategy in selling an idea is the preparation of a fully developed implementation plan designed to uncover many of the potential, hidden objectives to idea approval, and which will force realism into recommendations as they are being prepared.

An effective implementation plan answers these questions:

- How should it be implemented?
- What should be changed and in what sequence?
- Who should do it?
- How long should it take?
- Is any deadline required?
- What is the implementation cost?
- What are the consequences of delay?

The key to successful implementation lies in placing work orders for the necessary actions to be performed in the normal routine of business. The VA team should plan what these first-action work orders will be, and who will be assigned the responsibility of seeing that they are prepared for funding, priority assignment, and approval. It is so easy to walk out of a fine presentation and have everyone forget to acknowledge that someone must act.

In many cases, after presentation of ideas by a VA team, the team is disbanded because their assignment is complete. The only thing left to fill this void is the implementation plan—an intangible thing with no ability to monitor itself.

Implementation progress must be monitored just as systematically as was the conduct of the VA study. It is the responsibility of management to ensure that implementation is actually achieved. Therefore, one additional part of the implementation plan should be to designate a person—by name—with the responsibility to monitor all deadline dates in the implementation plan.

CHAPTER 11

Voice of the Customer

I need your support, I need your expertise, I need your
input, and most importantly, I need your money.

- POLITICIAN GREGG STILLSON – (MARTIN SHEEN)

No truer words were ever spoken. Those of us who make things,
design systems, and create procedures think we determine the
value in what we do. Wrong!

The user—the customer—determines value when he or she
acquires or uses what you produce. So don't deceive yourself.
The customer is always right!

***

Many businesses and agencies have requirements to consider:
economic, social, and environmental goals in balance with the
needs of their work. In order to achieve this balance, customer

stakeholder and public involvement is needed to help make decisions that are in their best interest.

A state agency[20] had a process to involve stakeholders in their decisions. A value-improvement study was conducted to review and recommend improvements to their existing Stakeholder Involvement Process (SIP) on a statewide basis, and then apply those findings to an actual project as a pilot.

The VA team reviewed the existing process and noted the following long list of issues and concerns:

- Lack of resources in planning
- Length of planning and design phases
- Changing stakeholders
- Agencies' unwillingness to be part of the process early
- Not perceived as a problem by management
- No one owns the process
- Lack of perceived value of stakeholders' early involvement
- Lack of political sensitivity
- Differences in involvement approaches between stakeholders and Caltrans
- Disconnect with the project development team and environmental/legal requirements
- Focus on legal requirements only
- Guide needed that is flexible enough to follow during different phases of the project
- Information provided in multiple locations
- Appears the current tools are not being used
- How to measure and monitor the stakeholder involvement plan?
- Number of stakeholders on complex projects can be substantial
- Stakeholders that need to be involved, and how they need or should be involved varies by issue and project phase

---

20 Sponsored by: California Department of Transportation (Caltrans), Conducted by: Laurie Dennis, PE, LEED AP, CVS–Life and Renee Hoekstra, CVS.

- Effectively engaging stakeholders on complex projects can be time and resource intensive

The team identified the functions of a stakeholder-involvement plan using active verbs and measurable nouns. This process allowed the team to truly understand all of the functions associated with the stakeholder-involvement plan process. As the functions were discussed, the team built its function model.

The team decided to brainstorm the following three functions, which seemed to be key to changing the process:

- **Define decision making**
- **Share information**
- **Identify stakeholders**

The ultimate goal of the project was to **establish buy-in** of the stakeholders. The team generated some eighty ideas to achieve the three desired functions.

The VA team developed performance attributes that were used to evaluate the ideas. These attributes were:

- **Improves adaptability**: An idea can be used on a project at any point in time, size, and complexity.
- **Improves project delivery**: Idea improves cost, scope (purpose and need), and schedule (reduces rework).
- **Improves decision making**: Idea improves internal and external decision making (where, when, who, and how a decision is made).
- **Implementable**: Idea is a viable approach and easy to implement.
- **Improves partnerships**: Idea develops and/or improves partnerships and relationships—both internal and external, with a focus on long-term relationships—and helps to build confidence and credibility.
- **Efficient use of resources**: Caltrans' resources related to time and money.

Ideas generated by the team were then evaluated by the team members to identify which ideas needed to be dropped from the idea list. The remaining ideas were combined with at least one of the sixteen prepared alternatives. The ideas represented a suite of opportunities to improve the SIP.

All of the ideas generated during the creative phase were recorded. A sample portion of the format is shown below.

The ideas were then scored relative to the performance attributes as follows, to prioritize them for further development and documentation. Those ideas with three to five votes meeting the attributes were then carried forward for further development. Those ideas receiving two votes or less were not.

Function – **Define decision making**

Number	Idea	Rank
01	Create a checklist to help decide if stakeholder plan is needed	0
02	Define the decision making plan with the stakeholders at the initial meeting, including an escalation plan	1
03	Prepare responsibility matrix with stakeholders	2
04	Prepare responsibility matrix with internal team	1
05	Establish project charter early for each project	1
06	Have each project prepare a formal project management plan	0
07	Clarify decision points for the process relative to types of projects	3

Function – **Share information**

01	Develop long term interagency relationships for mutual benefit	0
02	Pursue interagency agreements	3
03	Identify person responsible for the interagency relationship	0
04	Include permitting agencies in PDT	0
05	Develop matrix contact list for external and internal potential users	4

During this first phase, the study team reviewed the existing Caltrans stakeholder involvement process and brainstormed alternatives for improvement based on selection criteria developed. This would ensure alternatives were implementable, cohesive, and efficient for use by the project managers and project development teams.

Of the ideas generated, sixteen resulted in alternatives or updates to existing processes, which would assist in the overall process of identifying stakeholders and addressing their issues and concerns early and continuously throughout project delivery. These included:

Idea	Title
1.0	Pursue Public Partnership Agreements
2.0	Update the matrix contact list for external and internal potential stakeholders
3.0	Assign a unit to be responsible to prepare the communications plan
4.0	Caltrans hires expertise for stakeholder involvement to serve as a resource at PDT level
5.0	Identify a technical expert as a resource to the PDT to assist in development of the stakeholder involvement plan
6.0	Add WBS/RBS code to the work plan for the development and maintenance of stakeholder involvement plan
7.0	Develop a range of tools to assist in sharing information with strategic focus
8.0	Conduct regular briefings with executive management and partner agencies
9.0	Develop single resource with all the stakeholder involvement information
10.0	Develop a training program for use of the new process
11.0	Conduct stakeholder analysis
12.0	Develop assessment tool for determining the level and timing for stakeholder involvement
13.0	Clarify decision points that occur through the life of the project and tie to stakeholder involvement plan
14.0	Review PID process and PID document
15.0	Develop guidelines for work plan resource estimates for specific stakeholder involvement activities
16.0	Conduct a facilitated workshop for developing the stakeholder involvement plan, using a multi-functional team

A second phase of the value study applied the proposed alternatives on a project as a pilot—the Santa Barbara County South Coast Route 101, High Occupancy Vehicle (HOV) project—a ten-mile, lane-widening project on Route 101 in southern Santa Barbara County. This phase was to assess and validate the stakeholder- and community-involvement alternatives. The project had been unable to move forward for years due to lack of consensus of stakeholders on the project objectives.

This project was estimated to cost in the hundreds of millions and involved a myriad of government, local, and community stakeholders. The project required coastal development permits from four local agencies. It also needed a clear vision for moving forward.

The project communications, stakeholder involvement, and public-outreach activities developed from the workshop for use throughout this pilot project helped the project manager identify tools, resources, expertise, and ownership needed for an SIP on his project. He presented these needs to the project sponsors, who joined the effort and agreed to provide the project manager with the resources needed to ensure the implementation of the SIP to help move the project forward successfully.

The Phase II process study allowed a specific project team, including the major financial stakeholder, to participate and help to develop the initial stakeholder and public-involvement plan using a focused workshop. The facilitated stakeholder plan development framework (Alternative 16 as shown above) allowed workshop attendees to identify and organize information about key stakeholders, decision makers, project decision points, times when project input and/or information dissemination is needed, and other factors as identified as critical to the plan. The information was then organized into a cohesive plan for stakeholder and public involvement.

This format provided a head start for receiving support on the SIP from the project sponsors, project team members, and involved local agencies. A number of key factors made this format beneficial for this particular project, and should also support other projects. First, the format allowed for adequate discussion and participation from key project disciplines and stakeholders. Second, the group used an impartial facilitator with professional facilitation skills and knowledge of the discussions that were necessary to develop a detailed Stakeholder and Public Involvement Plan. Participation by the project sponsor and other partner jurisdictions (if appropriate) also helped to ensure that all necessary information was brought to the attention of the team and included in the plan as needed.

In addition, the format included a clear and concise workshop agenda, which identified the various topics and time frames during which the plan elements would be discussed. Tools proposed during Phase I of the study and used during this pilot project study included:

- Project charter
- Responsibility matrix for stakeholders and Caltrans divisions
- Issue resolution plan
- Project goals
- Communication matrix for stakeholder and public communication and input
- Stakeholder and public engagement matrix

This format for developing a Stakeholder and Public Involvement Plan provided a head start for receiving support on the stakeholder involvement plan from the project sponsors, project team members, and involved local agencies.

Continuing the collaborative-meeting process with the other stakeholder partners to finalize the plan will keep all stakeholders and the public informed, alleviate misunderstandings, allow the entire team to speak with one voice, and get decisions made at the right time in the process with the right individuals — thus saving time, cost, and frustration.

Resulting benefits from the VA study were:

- Tools developed for the SIP process
- A process adaptable to a project at any point in time, of any size and complexity
- A process that improves consistency
- User-friendly process
- Enhanced project delivery
- Identifiable decision points and types of decisions required

- Understandable resources - time and efficiency requirements
- A clear understanding of roles and responsibilities

Lessons learned from the pilot project included the following:

- Formal agreements with partner agencies are beneficial for getting and maintaining commitments.
- Regular meetings and briefings with executive management help to keep others informed.
- Regular briefings with executive management from partner agencies are beneficial to keep stakeholder partners informed.
- Opinion surveys to capture overall views can help the team focus their efforts and resources or identify needed change.
- There is a need for frequent updates to media, elected officials, community, and agency management.
- It is helpful to present concepts from a "What's in it for you" (WIIFY) perspective
- Getting "ownership" from elected officials is necessary.
- Getting "ownership" from communities is necessary.
- Strong departmental leadership is needed.
- Strong local champions are needed.
- Customized "tool boxes" are useful.

The effective dynamics of VA as a communications tool has always shown to produce a compendium of consensus from disparate parties. This is a real timesaving benefit for a complex and controversial stalled project.

CHAPTER 12

Collecting Money

In most companies, you don't get too much mail where people are saying, 'Hey, we lost this account.' But that's what you really need to know about, because it might change what you're doing.

- BILL GATES

Always remember that the customer determines value, not the company or the agency.

Collecting money owed involves a billing process. Do you think that is worth $28.75 a customer to collect it? No matter how much money you are collecting, $2.40 per month per bill sent out is too much money. That is how this study got selected for value analysis.

A gas utility company[21] with approximately 320,000 customers was reading and estimating meter quantity consumption and sending out monthly bills.

The first task of the study team was to prepare an estimate of the cost of the current method of collecting cash for their company. Labor cost for the time of all personnel involved in the operation was obtained, along with the costs for materials and supplies used, equipment leased, and overhead rates. The team, having defined all the functions of the process, then allocated cost to them.

This analysis revealed several value mismatches to be addressed in the study:

- Less than 5% of the cost of the system went to **collect payment**.
- More than 25% of the system cost went to pay for the **satisfy user**, **assure dependability**, **assure convenience**, and **attract user** functions.
- Approximately 40% of the **ensure accuracy** of the meter reading is caused by the need to reread a misread meter.

Talking to the customers about the problem and getting the voice of the customer (VOC) is always desired. To enhance the information phase, a customer attitude study was performed. This revealed:

- On a scale of 1–10, with 1 not being a serious fault, and 10 being most serious, customers ranked estimated billing as receiving an 8.
- Customers negatively interpreted the company budget plan as "you're using our money."
- The billing format was viewed as too complex to understand and too impersonal.

---

21 Sponsor: Midwest Utility Company, Conducted by: Tom Cook, CVS, FSAVE.

FUNCTIONS	FUNCTION/COST (in thousands of dollars)			
Process Request	$ 302			
Determine Consumption	$ 2,531			
Estimate Consumption		$ 99		
Read Meter		$ 2,441		
Record Reading			$ 2,417	
Change Chart			$ 24	
Calculate Bill	$ 317			
Render Bill	$ 1,085			
Collect Payment	$416			
Record Payment	$ 2,141			
Deposit Cash		$ 238		
Update File		$ 359		
Record Uncollectible		$ 1,544		
Satisfy User	$ 642			
Create Goodwill		$ 371		
Encourage Communication			$ 107	
Disseminate Information			$ 107	
Assist Customer			$ 157	
Answer Questions		$ 301		
Assure Dependability	$ 1,242			
Assure Accuracy		$ 285		
Assure Return		$ 801		
Check Credit			$ 69	
Prevent Losses			$ 712	
Motivate Payment				$ 484
Collect Bad-Debts				$ 248
Assure Reasonableness		$ 44		
Report Problems		$ 103		
Satisfy Rules		$ 9		
Assure Convenience	$ 369			
Simplify Collection		$ 264		
Simplify Payment		$ 105		
Offer Budget			$ 17	
Enclose Envelope			$ 26	
Offer Collections			$ 62	
Attract User	$ 35			
Communicate Image		$ 35		
Obtain Cash	$ 9,150			

Based on the above, the study team focused on value improvement to the **determine consumption** and **render bill** functions that represented approximately 40% of the cost of the system.

Thirteen proposals were developed. Three of these were implemented immediately at little or no cost. Nine proposals were called Class II because they would take up to one year to implement and required some investment to achieve. One proposal was called Class III because it relied on the development of future technology.

The total implementation cost of $459,645 in the first year would yield an ROI of $4.90 for each dollar invested in the first year. That is a breakeven period of 2.5 months in the first year.

In following years, the hard savings into the future will be 24.5% of the operating cost of the old billing system.

In addition to the tangible cost benefits, the following intangible benefits were obtained:

- A means to reduce the theft of gas
- Reduce in errors in meter reading
- Reduce unprocessed mail delivery
- Reduce customer complaints
- Motivate customers to budget
- Reduce bad-debt collections
- Provide favorable low-cost advertising space
- Respond to customer concerns

✳✳✳

Very often, value studies originate because you don't have enough money. This happened to me when I sold my old house and bought a new one.[22]

The old home had wall-to-wall carpeting in the living room. When I moved the furniture, I could see discoloration where the furniture had been. Because it was wall-to-wall carpet, it was not likely that it would fit the room dimensions of the new home. To make matters worse, in order to show the house for sale, I had to

---

22 Study example from Donald Parker

spend money to clean the old carpeting only to leave it behind. That is really terrible value.

The new house was a split-level home with hardwood flooring in the living room, hall, and three bedrooms. According to my wife, the baseline for carpeting the new home was wall-to-wall. We had it in our old home and felt to do less in the new home would be a downgrade in our quality of life. We needed it for the kids' running around. However, I could quickly see we could hardly afford the quantity needed—1,500 square feet. This is the layout of our 10'x15' living room.

The cost to carpet just this one room was more than $840. I didn't even want to estimate what the whole house would cost. I'd always been told that VA was a problem-solving methodology, and I had a problem!

I had done the information phase of looking at wall-to-wall carpeting—getting the price and all. Now I was on to the function phase.

To perform VA we had to define the basic function of the carpeting. Carpeting serves quite a number of functions, such as:

- **Minimize static**
- **Insulate floor**
- **Add color**
- **Protect surface**
- **Reduce slipping**
- **Permit removal**
- **Absorb sound**

We knew our first purpose for purchasing it was to **reduce noise** of the kids running around on the bare floors. When we asked how one could **reduce noise**, our answer was **cushion footsteps**.

We judged the worth of **cushioning footsteps** was about $22 if you issued everyone slippers. We laughed at this. Trying to keep slippers on the kids seemed impractical, and could we really demand that all our guests wear them too?

Then came the next mind-boggling thing. We asked, "How can you **cushion footsteps**? Why, you have to **locate footsteps** first!" Alas, we realized there are two locations in a room that

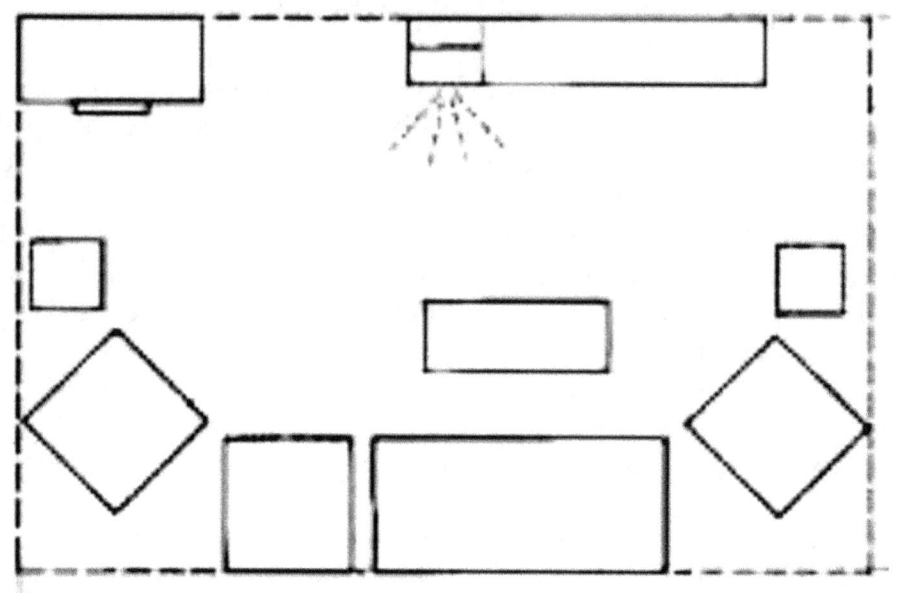

	Area	Meas.	Material	Labor	OH&P		Total
Carpet Pad	16.67	SY	$ 2.62	$ 2.10	$ 1.21	$	98.83
28 oz. Nylon Level Loop Carpet	16.67	SY	$ 28.00	$ 4.20	$ 4.30	$	608.33
Premium for <500 sf Full Roll		SY	25%		25%	$	134.58

Total Budget $ 841.75

After making a list of more than a dozen ways to cushion footsteps, the solution we settled on seemed natural: an area rug. The only place the kids' feet needed cushioning was in the center of the room. We could build bridges to **connect space** at the doorways with throw rugs that go from room to room.

Our function-inspired solution was to purchase a 6'x9' area rug for the living room. This had many benefits:

- It reduced the carpet needed from 150 square feet to 54 square feet.
- It reduced the size of the pad, if needed.
- It eliminated the need for paid labor to install — I could do it!
- It retained the beauty of the surrounding hardwood floor. We could take it with us if we ever moved again.

✳✳✳

A couple of months later I was an after-dinner speaker at a contractor's meeting. I was speaking on VA and I told the above carpet story as an example.

One contractor in the back of the room spoke up. "Mr. Parker, I thought you told me that in value analysis you life-cycle-costed everything," he said.

I said, "That's right — our measure of economic value is life-cycle cost."

The contractor said, "You didn't life-cycle cost your carpet solution."

I said, "What do you mean?"

He said, "Well, you have to have two sets of equipment to maintain it: buffer equipment to take care of the hardwood and vacuum equipment for the carpet. I'll bet you didn't life-cycle cost that!"

My response, "The hell you say. How much an hour do you think my wife gets?"

After the roar of laughter subsided, I continued on to tell them that we already had both sets of equipment in case they were needed; that I wasn't about to get into how often my wife cleaned; and that the user, my wife, approved the change and wasn't worried about it. The difference in our life-cycle cost for this was nil, and I couldn't see any increased out-of-pocket expenditures for making this change.

The story ended when I told them that one of the ideas on our list was to purchase a remnant carpet, which is a cheap piece cut off and left over from a larger roll. I said we could bind the edges and use it. I called it my "Rembrandt," as a play on words. My wife had fits and said that we would look cheap when guests came over.

To provide a little more "sell function," I offered to buy her a real 6'x9' oriental rug for the living room if we could purchase imitation machine-made oriental rugs for the dining room and each bedroom. She was very excited at that compromise.

In the end, the only area in our new home where we put wall-to-wall carpeting was on the stairs and in the hall. We had to **cushion footsteps** all the way there!

In the years we've lived in the house, the only carpet we've had to replace was the stair and hallway carpet. All the area rugs are still there, serving us well and increasing in value.

Epilogue

Every day when I came to work I met employees on the elevator who asked, "Have you saved any money?" My reply was always, "Not a damn thing. Have you done any better?"

We had two economists on the staff of the Public Buildings Service[23] who were looking at the stock market every day and working on the "Oil Depletion Allowance, the Trade Deficit, and the Balance of Payments" for the United States. I wondered what that had to do with our agency.

They too, asked me if I saved any money and I told them of a few specific changes made in our projects. Then I asked them, "Are you saving any money? What will you report to the commissioner as the benefit of your work?"

One replied, "I don't know, but it will be a big one!"

The moral of this story — we should all be working on what matters. And what matters is what can get done! VA really helps in what matters.

---

23 An agency of the General Services Administration.

Tools

There are tools of the trade to help you conduct and document your VA work if you choose to do it in-house. Most VA consultants can bring these to you.

1. A computer disc containing MS Word and Excel templates with worked examples and instructions for use is available from SAVE International under publications for Education & Training. The website link for these "Value Technology Templates" (catalogue number: 1094066920) is: http://www.value-eng.org/education_publications_bookstore.php#4 Included are templates for:

    > FAST customer
    > FAST technical
    > Life-Cycle Costing
    > Space Modeling
    > Value Index — Building
    > Value Index — Highway
    > Value Index — Manufacturing
    > Weighted Evaluation

2. The **Function iTool** is an online tool to help with function analysis. It is accessible by clicking on the Function iTool box in the upper right corner of the Miles Value Foundation website. The tool includes basic and secondary functions

for many products, services, and construction. It allows you to either:

- Enter a verb–noun function and get a list of ideas that achieve that function
- Enter an item and obtain the basic and secondary function it performs.

The web site link for the Function iTool is: http://www.valuefoundation.org/functions/index.htm

3. "How to" books and publications are available from the SAVE International website. The website link for this is: http://www.value-eng.org/education_publications_bookstore.php

www.ingramcontent.com/pod-product-compliance
Lightning Source LLC
Chambersburg PA
CBHW071231170526
45165CB00003B/1066